What did the Greeks think of cunnilingus? What was the opinion of the Romans concerning masturbation? These and many other questions are answered for the first time in the actual words of men who lived during those times. There are quotations from Ovid, author of The Art of Love, from Petronius, Suetonius, the Roman historian who related all the scandalous details of the sordid actions of the Roman Emperors (passages which are ordinarily left in the original Latin and not translated. All in all, there are about 150 authors consulted—many, never before translated into English.

This is a book for the layman. The reader need not sit with a Latin dictionary and an encyclopedia, looking up foreign phrases and obscure passages. Now, the reader will understand why the scholars grin when they mention Martial and Ausonius. Here, gathered in the only revised and corrected edition of Forberg's masterpiece of erotic activity through the ages.

F. K. FORBERG

DE FIGURIS VENERIS

THE
MANUAL
OF
CLASSICAL EROTOLOGY

LITERALLY TRANSLATED FROM THE LATIN

PARIS

MCMVII

WITH AN INTRODUCTION BY
MILTON VAN SICKLE

AN ORIGINAL HOLLOWAY HOUSE EDITION
HOLLOWAY HOUSE PUBLISHING CO.

PUBLISHED BY:
HOLLOWAY HOUSE PUBLISHING COMPANY
8060 Melrose Avenue, Los Angeles, California 90046

DISTRIBUTED BY:
ALL AMERICA DISTRIBUTORS CORPORATION
8431 Melrose Place, Los Angeles, California 90069

FIRST PRINTING 1967

Printed in the United States of America

CONTENTS

DE FIGURIS VENERIS

EDITOR'S INTRODUCTION

This book has been known by several titles: The Manual of Classical Erotology and De Figuris Veneris —which some have translated as The Metamorphosis of Venus. Indeed, calling it this is indicative of the timidity of the previous translators, for, while it may, in its passive sense, be translated as Concerning the Figure of Venus (or perhaps Concerning the Beauty of Venus), every Roman was aware that Venus was not only the goddess of—but also was identical to—sexual love. Thus, a more aggressive translation would be Concerning the Style of Sexual Love, or, loosely, Concerning the Variety of Sexual Love—for that is what this book is about.

The first publication of DE FIGURIS VENERIS occured in 1824 (in Latin, with a few words and phrases in Greek), as a supplement to the HER-MAPHRODITUS of Antonius Panoramitanus—which is explained in greater detail in the Introduction to the 1907 Paris Edition. The little which is known of the

author, Friedrich Karl Forberg, is contained in the
same Introduction. But, it may be of interest to point
out that Forberg led a sedentary life: He seems to
have ventured no more than 80 miles distance during
his lifetime; the towns where he was born, studied,
taught, worked and died all being within the Saxon
parts of Thuringia. All these towns are now in the
German Democratic Republic (East Germany) except
Coburg, which is now in West Germany.

It is rather amusing to note that Ernest, the Duke of
Saxe-Coburg (Coburg was the capital of the tiny,
autonomous duchy) at the time of Forberg's appoint-
ment to the library of Coburg—the same who was
duke at the time of the publication of this book—was
the father of Prince Albert, who later married Queen
Victoria. Moreover, the sister of this same Duke Ernest was the mother of Queen Victoria, but Duke
Ernest seems not to have held with the sentiments of
censorship and inspidity shared by so many of the
following generations—or perhaps he just didn't read
Latin and was unaware of the nature of Forberg's
work.

What Forberg has done in DE FIGURIS VENERIS
is to collect many of the statements of the Romans and
Greeks concerning various methods of sexual expression. He has not limited himself to the classical
writers, however, but has made occasional use of early
Medieval writers as well as a few from the Renaissance and some more recent. Forberg has separated
his book into eight sections, each dealing with a
particular mode of sex. He treats these methods de-
scriptively rather than analytically, and he thus would

appear to be less scientific than the analysts of our own time. But, certainly, we must give him credit for an honest and straightforward interest in the subject of sex, and, except for the section "On Cunnilingues," where we may detect condemnation and horror, his attitude is quite mature and free from hypocrisy. In contrast, the objectivity of the analysts is generally so extreme that the more they write about the subject of sex, the less we know about it—despite their use of case histories. This is probably because the material on which they base their publications is gathered under clinical conditions, while sexual expression doesn't ordinarily occur in such aseptic environments. So that, what they write bears little resemblance to the human condition. Moreover, the learned analysts invariably write of pathological occurences, but, nowhere in this book is there any suggestion that any of the subjects are pathological or abnormal (in the modern usage of these terms). Uncommon, perhaps— and very often not the types of behavior Forberg himself would care to be involved in—but, as our author might have cited Seneca: There is no dispute concerning taste.

Forberg first treats of copulation—this being the most popular form of sexual expression. He describes some of the numerous positions which have been used by specific people on certain occasions, drawing on Ovid, Suetonius and others.

Using most of the limited sources obtainable by us today, Forberg has given us a fairly thorough delineation of copulative activities in the human animal. He does not pretend to give us a complete picture of any

age or civilization—though he occasionally makes
some comment on the activities of Rome or Greece.
But it is generally the subject itself (copulation, etc.)
which interests him, rather than the mores or license
of any particular time or place.

Forberg then goes on to treat separately of sodomy,
fellatio, masturbation, cunnilingus, lesbianism, bestia-
lity and orgies. That he does not reserve special
chapters for sadism and masochism (and how many
other anomalies have we "discovered" other than
those covered in this work?), is undoubtedly because
these behaviors had not been invented as categories
(though, they certainly had been practiced). Which
might stand as an argument against the popular con-
ception of the depravity of former generations. But,
more likely, it points up our modern propensity for
excessive categorization—isolating and labeling each
aspect of sexual expression, and thereby, losing the
gestalt, the overall sense of the subject.

DE FIGURIS VENERIS, as it has come down to
us, is full of mistakes. Apparently, there has been only
one English translation of this work: that printed for
Viscount Julian Smithson in 1884 (which, according to
Legman was actually printed by Charles Carrington
in 1899). There is also a Paris edition of 1907, but the
text, except for a few minor corrections, is identical to
the text of 1884 edition. The 1884 edition also contains
enface the original Latin text, but this, like the translation, is a mass of errors.

However, I cannot help but feel that these errors
are entirely due to poor proofreading—this allowing
many typographical mistakes to creep in—and to the

faulty (and timid) translating. For example, the translator (whose name appears nowhere in the text) has
introduced the single quotation from Livy as "the rape
of the Sabines," which is the famous abduction of the
Sabine women by the Roman men which occured
(according to Livy) shortly after the foundation of the
city of Rome in 753 BC (Livy, I, 8). The incident
quoted by Forberg is the abduction of some Roman
prostitutes by visiting Sabine men, and it occurred in
501, soon after the foundation of the Republic (Livy,
II, 18).

Another example is a quotation from the META-
MORPHOSES of Apuleius. The transation by W.
Adlington in 1566 has been recently issued in a revised edition. A selection from Book III reads: "Thus
as we reasoned together the courage of Venus assailed
as well our desires as our members; and so she unar-
rayed herself and came to me, and we spent the night
in pastime and dalliance, and Fotis giving me all that
she might and more ..."

In the 1884 and in the 1907 editions of DE FI-
GURIS VENERIS, this same passage reads: "While
we were thus prattling, a mutual desire invaded our
minds and roused our limbs; having undressed entirely we gave ourselves up to the transports of Venus. I
soon felt tired. Fotis of her own good-will offered me
the catamite corollary."

They were not reasoning together or prattling, however, but bickering; and the Latin very distinctly
states that, having thrown off all garments, "we revelled nakedly in sexual delights." And the last line
reads: "Fotis with her characteristic affability thrust

upon me the 'gift of young boys' (literally: boyish gift)," meaning that she gave her buttocks for him to sodomize.

Also Martial's *Epigram* 98 of Book XIII, in which Martial tells his wife not to torment herself about his boy lovers because they give what she can not. She then offers him her buttocks, to which, Martial replies (according to English translation): "But it is not the same thing, I want a fig not an orange, and you must know theirs is a fig, yours an orange." Which, to me, is rather a perplexing simile. What the Latin actually says is that theirs is a *chia*, yours is a *marisca*. Chia being a sharp, pungent fig, while marisca is a fig which, though very sweet when young, is also very coarse-grained. And Martial certainly must have intended a pun here, for *mariscae* is the Latin for hemorrhoids. But the previous translation ignores such subtleties.

Another example is the translation of Juvenal's *Satire* VI, lines 195-6, as: "How well a soft and libertine voice will erect your member; it is as good as fingers!" What Juvenal actually says—and Forberg quotes him correctly—is: "When a seductive voice is worthless and will not excite your member—the fingers do it."

A great many of the citations are faulty, also. Where possible, these have been corrected—for I would hope that at least some of the readers will wish to go to the original sources, if only to read some of the interesting sections which Forberg could have included, but omitted for some reason.

I have everywhere endeavored to simplify tangled sentence structure, replace timid euphemisms with a more accurate translation from the Latin, and I have added quite a few footnotes—in addition to those already included by Forberg, the few added by the translator and those of the editor of the 1907 edition —thinking that it might be of some interest to the reader to know something about the people mentioned by Forberg. The footnotes of Forberg and the translator are numbered, those of the editor of the 1907 edition are in brackets, and my footnotes are identified by letters. So, anyone wishing to take exception will know whom to blame. Greek words have been rendered here into Roman letters (how many people read Greek, today?) except in Epigram CXXVIII of Ausonius where the shapes of the letters are important.

This edition is, then, I believe, smoother, more readable—and much more accurate, than any previous English edition.

Milton Van Sickle

INTRODUCTION TO 1907 PARIS EDITION

The eminent Author of this book never became
famous. His name is mentioned occasionally in connection with the "Hermaphroditus" of Antonio Beccadelli, known by the surname of Panormitanus, which
he edited. Brunet, Charles Nodier, and the *Bibliogra-
phie des Ouvrages relatifs aux Femmes, a l'Amour et
au Mariage*, speak of him in this connection; while a
list of his works appears moreover in the *Index Lo-
cupletissimus Librorum* or *Bücher-Lexicon* (Bibliogra-
phical Lexicon) of Christian Gottlob Kayser, Leipzig,
1834. But with the exception of the *Allgemeine
Deutsche Biographie*, the publication of which was
commenced in 1878 by the Historical Commission of
the Munich Academy, and which has devoted a short
notice to him, all Dictionaries and Collections whether
of Ancient or of Modern Biography are mute with
respect to him.

The *Conversations-Lexicon* and the vast Encyclo-
paedia of Ersch and Gruber do not contain a single

line about him, while Michaud, Didot, Bachelet and
Dezobry, Bouillet, Vapereau, utterly ignore his existence. For all that he well deserves a word or two.

Friedrich Karl Forberg was born in the year 1770 at
Meuselwitz, in the Duchy of Saxe-Altenburg, and died
in 1848 at Hildburghausen. He was a philosopher and
a collaborator with Fichte, while he devoted a part of
his attention to religious exegesis: but above all he
was a philologian, and a humanist,—at once learned
and inquisitive.

He followed first the career of a University-teacher;
Private-docent in 1792, Assistant Professor in the Fa-
culty of Philosophy at Jena (1793), he was installed in
1796 as Co-Rector at Saalfeld. His inaugural thesis:
"Dissertatio inauguralis de aesthetica transcendentali,"
is dated 1792 (Jena, 8vo.); this was followed by a
"Treatise on the Original Conditions and Formal Li-
mitations of Free Will" in German, and an "Extract
from my Occasional Writings" also in German (1795).
From 1796 to 1800 he wrote extensively in defence of
the teachings of Fichte in Journals, Reviews, particularly in the Philosophical Magazine of Schmid, and in
sundry publications emanating from Fichte himself.
He published moreover: "Animadversiones in loca se-
lecta Novi Testamenti," (Saalfeld, 1798, 4to.), "An
Apology for his Pretended Atheism," in German
(Gotha, 1799, 8vo.). "Obligations of Learned Men," in
German (Gotha, 1801, 8vo.), etc.

The second part of his life seems to have been
devoted entirely to Literature. In 1807 he was appointed as Conservator of the Aulic Library at Coburg, and having had enough of philosophy, he turned
his whole attention to the study of Latin and Greek
antiquity. Previously to this his tastes had already

been revealed by the publication of several pretty
editions of the minor Latin erotic poets; these form a
collection of six or eight volumes in 16mo., with red
margin-lines, and are now very difficult to procure.

The discovery he made in the Coburg Library of a
manuscript of the "Hermaphroditus" of Panormitanus,
offering important new readings and variants from the
received text, suggested the idea to him of producing
a definitive edition of the work, with copious commentaries.

The said "Hermaphroditus," so called, "because,"
says La Monnoye, "all the filth in connection with
both sexes forms the theme of the volume," is a
collection of Latin Epigrams filled out with a patch-
work of quotations from Virgil, Ovid and Martial, in
which memory has a much larger share than imagination, and which has never appeared to us to possess
any great literary value. But the mishaps the book has
had to encounter, its having been publicly burnt in
manuscript in the market places of Bologna, Ferrara
and Milan, the anathemas hurled against it by some
savants, and the favour with which it was received by
others, who were glad to awaken by its persual old
reminiscences, have given it a kind of reputation. The
Abbé Mercier de Saint-Léger was the first to publish it
in Paris, together with the works of four other poets of
the same sort: Ramusius de Rimini, Pacificus Maximus, Jovianus Pontanus, and Joannes Secundus (1).

_____

(1) Quinque illustrium Poetarum, Antonii Panormitae; Ra-
mussi Ariminensis; Pacific Maximi Asculani Io. Joviani
Pontani; Io. Secundi Hagiensis, Lusus in Venerem, partim
ex codicibus manuscriptis, nunc primum editi Parisiis,
prostat ad Pristrinum, in Vico suavi, (at Paris, at Molini's,
rue Mignon), 1791, 8vo.

But Forberg, whilst fully appreciating the work and
particularly the courage of the learned Frenchman,
found much to find fault with; the Epigrams of Panormitanus were not numbered, which made citations
from them troublesome, a great number of readings
were faulty, and, thanks to his manuscript, he could
correct them; lastly, Mercier de Saint-Léger had omitted to give any running commentary on his author, to
explain his text by means of notes and the comparison
of parallel passages, whereas according to Forberg a
book of this character required notes by tens and
hundreds, each verse, each hemistich, each word,
offering matter for philosophical reflections and highly
interesting comparisons. He therefore took the book in
hand and began to collect with inquisitive care everything the ancients had written upon the delicate subjects treated in the "Hermaphroditus."

But having come to the end of his task, he found
that his commentary would drown the book, that
hardly would he be able to get in a verse of it every
two or three pages, all the remainder of the book
being taken up by his notes, and that the result would
be chaos. Dividing his work into two parts, he left the
smaller one in the shape of annotations, reduced to the
merest indispensable explanations, to the "Hermaphroditus," while of the second and more copious harvest
of his erudite researches he composed a special treatise,
which he had printed as a supplement under the title,
"Apophoreta," or "Second Course"; this treatise being
in his eyes only a kind of dessert, following upon the
substantial repast furnished by the Latin Poet of the
15th century. The whole forms a volume much sought

after by amateurs: "Antonii Panormitae *Hermaphrodi-tus*; primus in Germania edidit et Apophoreta adjecit Frider. Carol. Forbergius. Coburgi, sumtibus Meuse-liorum, 1824, 8vo." (2).

Forberg, good, simple man, was mistaken, owing to his too great modesty; the true feast, at once substantial, nourishing and savoury, is his own work, the work which he elaborated from his own resources, from his inexhaustible memory and from his astonishing knowledge of the Greek and Latin authors down to their minutest details. On reprinting this excellent work, which undoubtedly deserved to be translated, we have given it a new title, that of "The Manual of Classical Erotology," one that is much more suitable than the old one. In virtue of the charm, the abundance, the variety of the citations, it is a priceless erotic Anthology; in virtue of the methodical classification of the contents Forberg has adopted, it is a didactic work,— a veritable Manual. He began with collecting from the Greek and Latin writers the largest number possible of scattered notices, which might serve for points of comparison with the Epigrams of Beccadelli; having possessed himself of a large accumulation of these, it occurred to him to set them out in order, arranging them in conformity with the similiarity of their contents, deciding finally upon a division into eight chapters, corresponding with the same number of special manifestations of the amorous fancy and its depravities:

---

(2) To certain copies are added some thirty engravings, representing the principal erotic postures; these engravings are taken from the *Monuments de la Vie privée des Douze Césars*, and from the *Monuments du Culte Secret des Dames Romaines*, two work, now becoming every day rarer.

I. — Of Copulation.
II. — Of Pederastia.
III. — Of Irrumation.
V. — Of Cunnilingues.
VI. — Of Tribads.
VII. — Of Intercourse with Animals.
VIII. — Of Spintrian Postures.
IV. — Of Masturbation.

He found that he had to make sub-divisions in each class according to the nature of the subject, to note particularities, individualities; and the contrast between this scientific apparatus, and the facetious matters subjected to the rigorous laws of deduction and demonstration is not the least amusing feature of the book. Probably no one but a German savant could have conceived the idea of thus classifying by categories, groups, genera, variations, species and sub-species, all known forms of natural and unnatural lusts, according to the most trustworthy authors. But Forberg pursued another aim besides. In the course of his researches he had noticed how reticent the annotators and expounders generally are in clearing up matters which would seem to require it the most, some in consequence of a false reserve, others for fear of appearing too knowing, and others again from ignorance; also how many mistakes and gross blunders they have fallen into, by reason of their not understanding the language of erotics and failing to grasp its infinite shades of meaning.

It is precisely on those obscure and difficult passages of the Ancient poets, on those expressions purposely chosen for their ambiguity, which have been the torment of the critics and the puzzle of the most

erudite commentators, that our learned Humanist
has concentrated his most convincing observations.

The number of authors, Greek, Latin, English,
French, German, Dutch, whom he has laid under
contribution in order to formulate his exact and judi-
cious classifications, mounts up to a formidable total.
There are to be found in *The Manual of Erotology*
something like five hundred passages, culled from
more than one hundred and fifty works, all classified,
explained, commented upon, and in most cases, enve-
loped in darkness as they had been, made plain as
light itself by the mere fact of juxtaposition. With
Forberg for a guide no one need henceforth fear to go
astray,—to believe, for instance, like M. Leconte de
Lisle, that the woman of whom Horace says that she
changes neither dress nor place, *"peccatve superne"* (3)
"has not erred beyond measure"; what a mistake!—or
with M. Nisard to translate Suetonius's expression
"illudere caput alicuius" (4) "to attempt someone's
life"!

Forberg, a philosopher, has treated these delicate
subjects like a philosopher, namely, in a purely specula-

_____

(3) See the 7th line on page 49. The mistake made by M.
Leconte de Lisle becomes at once apparent, for it is
evident that to translate the passage in question as meaning "has not erred beyond measure" is nonsense, the real
maning being "never had sinned *above*," which being
interpreted means, she had never copulated in the posture
known as that of "The Horse of Hector."
(4) Seen Note 67 on page 120. Here again M. Nisard's
mistake also becomes apparent. The passage in question
does not mean "to attempt someone's life"; its correct
meaning being "to assault the heads," which interpreted
means, he irrumated in mouths.

tive manner, as a man quite above and beyond terres-
trial matters, and particularly so with respect to the
lubricities which he has made it his task to examine so
closely. He declares he knows nothing of them per-
sonally, has never thought of making experimental in-
vestigations on them, but derives all his knowledge
from books. His candour is beyond suspicion. He has
not escaped censure; but having a reply ready for
every objection and authorities to quote on every
point, he found an answer to his detractors ready-made
in the phrase of Justus Lipsius, who had been reproached with taking pleasure in the abominations of
Petronius: "The wines you set upon the table excite
the drunkard and leave the sober man perfectly calm;
in the same way, this kind of reading *may* very likely
inflame an imagination already depraved, but it makes
no impression upon a mind that is chaste and dis-
ciplined."

AUTHORS PREAMBLE

AUTHORS PREAMBLE

We propose to pass in review the various methods of sexual love,—though truly not all of them. For how is it possible to specify the thousand modes (1), the thousand forms of Love, on which the inventive satiety of pleasure ventures? But at any rate such as fall into distinct and definite kinds admit of being easily

(1) Ovid (a) (*Art of Love*, I, 435, 36):
"To fully expose the ungodly wiles of harlots, ten mouths, and as many tongues to boot, would not suffice."
Luisa Sigea, (*Dialogue* VI) (b): "The body in sacrificing to Venus can take as many postures as there are ways in which it can bend and curve. It is equally impossible to enumerate all these as it is to say which is best fitted to give pleasure. Each acts in this respect according to his own caprice, according to place, time, and so on, choosing the one he prefers. Love is not identical for each and all."
(a) Ovidius Naso (43 BC-17AD) Roman poet who spent the last 8 years of his life in exile because of some "minor" (and unknown) incident. *Ars Amatoria* (The Art of Love) was published about 2BC.
(b) Aloisia Sigaea (Luisa Sigea) (1530-1560). Born at Toledo of a French father Jacques Sigée), she knew Latin, Greek, Hebrew, Arabic and Syriac. She was supposedly the author of *Satirae Sotadicae de arcanis Amoris et Veneris*, but see note S.

and methodically classified. Do not, inquisitive reader,
hope for more than this. We are not of those who seek
after a petty personal glory by unveiling the results of
their own experience or by describing novel *tours de
force* in the wrestling-school; we are not so much as
raw recruits at this game. Nor yet is it our intention to
reveal things we have seen or heard in this connection.
If we *would*, we could not, to your satisfaction, for
books are our only authorities.

We are solely and entirely bookmen, and scarcely
frequent our fellow creatures at all.

These trifles engaged our attention first as a mere
pastime. We were led to them accidentally, as we
roamed from subject to subject; for Philosophy, the
garden we had hoped to set up our tent in for life, lies
desolate. How *can* Philosophy flourish in times like
ours, when almost every new day sees new systems
sprout forth, to die down again tomorrow; when there
are as many philosophers as philosophies, when
schools have ceased to exist, when instead of groups
only individuals are to be met with? Our second
motive was to provide some satisfaction, however
little, to the claims of those readers who very often
find themselves disconcerted by the unconventional
raciness of Ancient authors and their out-spoken witticisms, and justly complain of the prudish brevity or
entire silence of the Commentators who leave their
difficulties unexplained. Of course these latter wrote
for the young; and no one can blame them under the
circumstances for not having dwelt carefully and cur-
iously on shameful secrets.

If we have fallen into any mistakes, lay the fault, we
beg, first on our insufficient intellectual furniture, se-

condly on our ignorance as to the more uncommon
forms of lust, an igorance prevalent in small towns,
and lastly, if you please, put it down to the honest
simplictiy of our Coburg citizens *members*. (c)

We only follow others' example. We have predecessors in Astyanassa, who according to Suidas (2) first
wrote "of Erotic Postures"; and in Philaenis of Samos
(3), or rather, to deprive no one of his due, Polycrates,

---

(2) Suidas (d) under *Astyanassa*: "Astyanassa, maid of
Helen the wife of Menelaus, who was the first to invent
the different positions in the act of love. She wrote "Of
Erotic Postures"; and was followed and imitated by Philaenis and Elephantis, who carried further the series of
suchlike obscenities."

(3) *Priapeia* (e) (LXIII): "To her a certain girl (I very
nearly gave her name) is wont to come with her paramour;
and if she fails to discover as many postures as Philaenis
describes, she goes away again still itching with desire."

Philaenis has found a champion of her good name in
Aeschrion of Samos who said that Polycrates The Sophist
wrote the work, and Aeschrion wrote an epitaph for her
that is still extant in Athenaeus (f) (VIII, 335): The last
lines read:

"I was not lustful for men nor lewd; but Polycrates, by
birth an Athenian, a mill-clapper of talk, a foul-tongued
sophist, wrote—of what he wrote, I know nothing at all."

Her works were familiar to Timarchus in Lucian (g)
(*Apophras*, p. 158, — vol. VII, of Works of Lucian, edit.
J. P. Schmid): "Tell me where you find these words and
expressions,—in what books? is it in the volumes of Philaenis, that are always in your hands?"

(c) This becomes a pun in translation. Forberg uses the
word *mentula*, about which there can be no doubt.

(d) Suidas was a Byzantine scholar living around 970AD.
He compiled a dictionary which, despite its faults, contains
a wealth of information not otherwise available.

an Athenian sophist, who brought out under the name
of that honorable matron a book "On the various
Postures of Love." Then there was Elephantis (4) or

_____

(e) *Priapeia* is a collection of 86 poems on the subject of
sexual love by various poets—probably from the time of
Augustus (30BC–14AD).
(f) Athenaeus (170-230AD), a Greek of Alexandria. His
Deipnosophistae The Sophists [or Doctors] at Dinner) is a
potpourri of learning (1500 works by 700 writers are
mentioned) and gossip. His book has also been called one
of the earliest cookbooks.
(g)   Lucian, born in Syria around 120 AD, spent much
of his life in Athens and became a prolific satirist.
(4) Suetonius (h) (*Tiberius*, ch. 43): "He decorated his
various and variously arranged sleeping-chambers with
pictures and bas-reliefs of the most licentious character,
and furnished them with the works of Elephantis, that no
one in performing should want a model of the posture
required."
Priapeia, (IV):
"Taking pictures from the licentious treatises of Elephantis, Lalage presents them an offering to the stiff-standing
god, and begs you prove if she performs agreeably to the
pictured postures."
It would seem then that artists depicted the postures
decribed by Elephantis, she herself possibly setting the
example. Paintings of the sort Lalage dedicates to Priapus,
and asks her lover to have her and see if she is a docile
pupil in faithfully imitating all the modes of connection
depicted in them. No doubt such representations of licentious postures, taken from the works of Elephantis or
Philaenis or elsewhere stimulated the ingenuity of Artists
to work out in emulation these enticing *motifs* to the
highest degree of finish. Ovid alludes to such works of art
in his *Art of Love* (II, 679-80):
"They unite in Love in a thousand postures; no picture
could suggest any fresh ones . . ."
as also the author of an ancient Epigram quoted by Joseph

Elephantine, a Greek girl, with whose licentious writings Tiberius is said to have furnished his sleeping-room; also Paxamus (5) who composed the *Dodeca-*

Scaliger (i) in his Commentary on the Priapeia (IV—III in the Scaliger edition):
"And when she has thrown herself into every posture in imitation of the seductive pictures, she may go: but let the pictures be left hanging over my bed."
Nothing was commoner with the Romans than to decorate the walls and partitions of rooms with licentious paintings, as may be gathered from Propertius (j) (II, vi, 27-30, 33-34):
"The hand that first painted filthy pictures, and exposed foul sights in an honest home, corrupted the pure eyes of young maids, and chose to make them accomplices of his own lubricity ... In old days our walls were not daubed with fancies of this vile sort, when never a partition was adorned with a vicious subject."
(h) Gaius Suetonius Tranquillus (about 70-145 AD), a Roman, best known for his *Lives of the 12 Caesars.* Also wrote *De Viris Illustribus,* but little of it has survived.
(i) Joseph Justus Scaliger (1540-1609). 10th child (3rd son) of Julius Caesar Scaliger (see note f, ch. IV). Born at Agen, he removed to Geneva in 1574 and to Leiden in 1590. He is known as a scholar of Latin, Greek; Arabic and Hebrew.
(j) Sextus Propertius (about 50-16 BC), Roman author of love poems of high quality.
(5) Suidas: "Paxamus wrote the *Dodecatechnon*; the subject is the obscene postures." But I think he has no good reason to connect with this the epithet *Dodecamechanos* given to a certain Cyrene. The said wanton damsel seems to have practised rather than described the twelve postures of Venus. Suidas under *Dodecamechanon*: "There was a famous *hetaera,* Cyrene by name, further known as *Dodecamechanos,* because she practised twelve different postures in making love."
Aristophanes (k) says in the *Frogs* (1325-28):
"Do you dare to criticise my songs, you that modulate your

technon on lascivious postures; and Sotades (6) of

---

cadences on the twelve-fold postures of Cyrene?"

Her names occurs also in the *Thesmophoriazusae* (98), but
merely her name. I am doubtful as to whether Musaeus
should be counted among writers on the Erotic postures.
Martial (1) (XII, 96) recommends Instantius Rufus to read
his (Museaus') books, as being of the most advanced
lasciviousness, vying with those of the Sybarites in obscenity and full of the most suggestive and spicy wit; warning
him at the same time to have his girl ready to hand, if he
did not want his hands to perform the wedding-march and
consummate the marriage without a woman at all.

(6) Athenaeus, (XIV, 620): "Also the *Ionicologos* is one
who recites the Ionic (i.e., licentious) poems of Sotades
and his predecessors, Alexander of Aetolia, Pyres of Miletus, Alexis (m) and others of that sort. The recitor is also
called *kinaidologos*. But in this *genre* the most eminent
writer is Sotades of Maroneia, as is stated by Carystius of
Pergamum in his work on Sotades, and by Apollonius,
Sotades' son, who also wrote a work on his father's poems.
His end was a miserable one. Having assailed Ptolemy
Philadelphus, King of Egypt, with witticisms too indepen-
dent for the sensitive ears of princes (n), the king caused
him to be enclosed in a leaden casket, and thrown into the
sea."

(k) Aristophanes (444-388 BC), Athenian author of come-
dies, some of which are still considered unsurpassed.

(1) Marcus Valerius Martialis (about 40-103AD), a Roman
poet of epigrams, born in Augusta Bilbilis Spain—hence
Forberg's occasional reference to him as 'our good friend
of Bilbilis.'

(m) Alexis (or perhaps, Alexas) is not otherwise known and
may be a mistake of the copyist, or he may be the Alexis
who died in 286 BC at the age of 106 and who was the
author of 245 plays which were similar to those of Aristophanes. Alexander of Aetolia lived at the court of Ptolemy
Philadelphus (285-246) and later at the court of Antigonus
Gonatus (276-239) of Macedonia. Pyres of Miletus is
unknown.

Maroneia, surnamed the Cinaedologue, from whose name a whole class of literature, remarkable for its excessive lubricity, is known as the Sotadic; and Sabellus, of whom Martial speaks (XII, 43):

"Copious verses, only too copious, on scandalous subjects you have read me, O Sabellus, such as neither the maids of Didymus (7) know, nor yet the wanton treatises of Elephantis. Therein are new postures of Love that the desperate fornicator tries, and what debauchees use, but never tell of,—how grouped in a series five copulate at once, how a greater number still

---

(n) Ptolemy of Egypt was called Philadelphus (lover of his sister) because, in 276, he married his maternal sister, Arsinoe. Such an alliance was acceptable to the Egyptians, but was considered scandalous by the Greeks (and Ptolemy was a Greek), although the Greeks accepted marriage between paternal siblings. Sotades remarked, "You are putting your member into a hole unholy."

(o) Lucius Annaeus Seneca (5 BC-65 AD), Roman philosopher, playwright and satirist, and also tutor of Nero, who ordered Seneca to commit suicide in 65.

(p) Didymus (63-?), Greek scholar from Alexandria who lived and taught at Rome; because of the volume of his work, he was known *Chalkenteros*, the man with the brass bowels.

(7) Who were these "maids of Didymus?" Nobody knows. Failing any more plausible supposition, it may very well be conjected that among the four thousand works written according to Seneca (o) (*Letter* LXXXVIII) by the Grammarian Didymus (p), there was one on the postures of lascivious girls, worthy to be named side by side with the treatises of Elephantis. Undoubtedly a man who devoted himself to such subtle questions as whether Anacreon was more libertine than drunkard, whether Sappho was a public woman or not, was quite likely to discuss the Erotic postures.

can make a chain. It was hardly worth the pains to be erudite."

Moreover amongst our predecessors was the famous Pietro Aretino (8), a man of an almost divine genius, whom ill-natured report represents as having illustrated sixteen plates painted by Julio Romano and engraved on copper by Marc-Antonio with verses indecent beyond all expression; Lorenzo Veniero again (9), a Venetian nobleman, author of a little work

---

(8) See Bayle's *Dictionnaire historique et critique* (Historical and Critical Dictionary), article: *Pierre Arétin;* also Murr's *Journal zur Kunstgeschichte* (Year-Book of the History of Art), vol. XIV, pp. 1-72. (q)

(q) Pietro Aretino (1492-1556). Born at Arezzo, Tuscany, he lived at Rome to 1523, then Milan, Tuscany, and finally remained at Venice after 1526. His "Luxurious Sonnets" were first published in 1523.

(9) Pierre Bayle, in his *Dictionnaire* under *Pierre Arétin;* "There is a *Dialogue between Maddalena and Giulia,* entitled *La Puttana Errante* (The Wandering Whore), in which are exhaustively treated *i diversi congrungimenti* (the different modes of intercourse), to the number of thirty-five. Aretino, though the book has always been printed under his name, disowns it, declaring it to be the work of one of his pupils named Veniero." Brunet, *Manuel du Libraire* (Book-dealer's Handbook). "The *Puttana Errante,* a little book, very rare, quite worthy of Aretino in view of the obscenities it contains, but which has been erroneously attributed to him. Lorenzo Veniero, a Venetian nobleman, is the real author. (r) He published it to avenge himself on a Venetian courtesan named Angela, whom he designates under the insulting name of Zaffetta, that is to say, in the Venetian dialect, daughter of a police-spy."

[Bayle, Forberg and many other writers have confused the *Puttana Errante,* a poem by Lorenzo Veniero and a burlesque parody of the Romances of Chivalry, with the *Dialo-*

in Italian, bearing the title *La Puttana Errante* (The
Wandering Whore), in which he has undertaken to
specify no less than thirty-five modes of loving. Lastly
there was Nicolas Chorier (s) a French lawyer, who
under the name of Luisa Sigea, a young Spanish lady,

---

gue between Maddalena and Giulia, a prose work to
which the Elzevirs gave the title properly belonging to the
poem. Neither one nor the other is the work of Pietro
Aretino. See note at end of vol. VI. of the *Dialogues du
divin Pietro Aretino* (Dialogues of the divine Pietro Aretino), Paris, Liseux, 1879, 3 vols. 8vo., and London, 1880,
3 vols 8vo. Note of French Translation of Forberg, *Manuel
de Erotologie Classique,* Paris, Liseux, 1882.]
[These "verses indecent beyond all expression" are nothing
less than Aretino's "Luxurious Sonnets!" The authenticity
or existence of both the Sonnets and the Posture Engravings has remained in doubt for centuries, but by the
accidental unearthing of an old manuscript copy of the
Sonnets, and of a complete set of the sixteen Posture
Engravings, the matter has now been definitely settled.
Julio Romano painted them, Marc-Antonio engraved them,
and Aretino wrote a Sonnet under each. An edition de luxe
of the Sonnets and Posture Engravings, both together, has
been privately published and is uniform with this present
volume. Note by the editor of the 1907 Paris edition de
luxe of *The manual of Classical Erotology.*]
(r) Lorenzo Veniero (or Venier) has not otherwise been
identified except as a secretary to Aretino. Three Venetian
Doges were of this family; others were governors and lords
of various Aegean islands (especially Kythera) until 1797.
More recent evidence suggests the author to be another
secretary of Aretino, Niccolo Franco.
(s) Nicolas Chorier (1612-96). A French lawyer of Vienne.
He published the work (known as, *The Dialogues of
Luisa Sigea*) in 1658 or '59, claiming it to be written in
Spanish by Luisa Sigea and translated into Latin by
Joannes Meursius. It is now generally agreed that Chorier
wrote it in Latin—and neither Sigea nor Meursius had
anything to do with it.

has given us the *Satirae Sotadicae de arcanis Amoris
et Veneris* (Sotadic Satires on the Secret Rites of Love
and Venus); though the book also appears under the
name of Joannes Meursius(t) with the title *Elegantiae
Latini Sermonis* (Graces of Latin Prose). In this book
you do not know which to admire most, the style at
once elegant, correct and careful, yet free from pe-
dantry, the wit equally gay and graceful, the brilliant
sparks of Latin erudition that glitter everywhere, the
rich and copious eloquence graced as with jewels by
polished and luminous words and phrases of a pleasant antique flavor, or lastly the pre-eminent skill
displayed in varying with such manifold versatility
one simple theme. The others we need not mention
further.

Our predecessors, whether the more modern, or
those of Antiquity whom we have cited, and all whose
works alas! envious time has robbed us of, did not lack
severe critics, nor yet studious readers. And our own
treatise will no doubt in its turn meet with both these
classes. It is a man's book; we have written it, fearless
of censure, for men—not for such as are wont with
frowning brow "to pitchfork nature out of doors," but
rather for such as have once for all dared to live their
lives, who neither wish to lurk in darkness nor yet to
defy the open day with effrontery, in one word for
those who think that in Love as in all else the golden
mean is the course to choose. Let others go their way,
and arrogate to themselves the title of sages!

(t) Joannes Meursius (1579-1639). Johannes Van Meurs, a
renowned scholar, was professor of Greek at Leiden from
1610 to 1625, when he moved to Denmark.

The work of Venus may be accomplished with or without the help of the mentula. If with the mentula, the friction of this organ, in which friction the whole pleasure consists, can be effected either in the vulva, in the anus, in the mouth, by the hand or in any cavity of the body. If without the mentula, the vulva may be worked either with the tongue, with the clitoris, or with any object resembling the virile organ.

OF COPULATION

CHAPTER ONE

OF COPULATION

And first of all let us consider what is accomplished by means of the mentula introduced into the vulva. This is, properly speaking, to effect copulation; but there are various ways of doing it. As a matter of fact copulation can be effected:—the man face downwards with the woman on her back, the man on his back with the woman face down, the man on his back with the woman turning her back to him; the man sitting with the woman turning her face towards him, sitting with the woman turning her back to him; the man standing or kneeling with the woman turning her face towards him, standing or kneeling with the woman turning her back to him. Let us examine each of these methods separately.

Coition with the man face down on the woman who lies on her back is the ordinary method, and the most natural.

Luisa Sigea says:

"For my own part I like the usual custom and the ordinary method best: the man should lie upon the

woman, who is on her back, breast to breast, stomach
to stomach, pubis to pubis, piercing her tender cleft
with his rigid spear. Indeed what can be imagined
sweeter than for the woman to lie extended on her
back, bearing the welcome weight of her lover's body,
and exciting him to the tender transports of a restless
but delicious voluptuousness? What more pleasant
than to feast on her lover's face, his kisses, his sighs,
and the fire of his wanton eyes? What better than to
press the loved one in her arms and so awake new fires
of desire, to participate in amorous sensations un-
blunted by any taint of age or infirmity? What more
favorable to the delight and enjoyment of both than
such tossing and flinging with lascivious movements?
What more opportune at the instant of dying a voluptuous death than to recover again under the revivify-
ing vigor of burning kisses? He who plies Venus on
the reverse side, satisfies but one of his senses, he who
does the same face to face satisfies them all." (*Dialogue* VI.)

Ovid, the Master of Love's Mysteries, invites pretty
women to take this posture by preference:

"See you reckon up each of your charms, and take
your posture according to your beauty.

One and the same mode does not become every
woman.

You are especially attractive of face; then lie on
your back." (*Art of Love*, III, 771-773.)

This posture is by no means limited to one mode.
The woman lying on her back, the rider may clasp her
between his legs, or she may receive him between
hers. Yet another position may be adopted, according
as the woman lie back with legs stretched wide apart

or with the knees raised.

It is this position,—lying on her back with legs wide
apart, that Caviceo asks Ottavia to assume for making
Love:

"I do not wish you." he says, "to work your buttocks,
or to respond with corresponding movements to my
efforts. Neither do I wish you to lift your legs up,
whether both at once, or one after the other, when I
have mounted you. What I do wish you to do is this:
first stretch your thighs far apart, open them as wide
as a woman well can. Offer your vulva to the member
which is going to pierce it, and without altering this
position, let *me* complete the work ... Count my
thrusts one by one, and see you make no mistake in
the total." (Luisa Sigea, *Dialogue* V).

Would you see a representation of this? Take the
tale *Félicia ou mes fredaines(a)*, part II, chap. XXV,
and look at the plate facing the text.

The other position, in which the woman is lying
with her knees raised, is the one which Callias makes
Tullia take:

"After I am lying upon your dear body," he says,
"press me fast in your arms, and hold me thus embraced. Draw your legs back as far as you can, so that
your pretty feet touch your buttocks, smooth as marble." (Luisa Sigea, *Dialogue* VI).

If you would enter the woman lying on her back
with her legs in the air, it may be done in yet another

_____

(a) Written by Andrea de Nerciat (1739-1801), French
author and playwright, *Félicia* is his major work. The
plates mentioned by Forberg are not in all editions.

way than Tullia's mode, and one perhaps still more
delicious, by placing your mistress so that she rests her
legs crossed over the loins of her rider. A representation of this very pleasant posture, which would rouse
the numbed verge of a Hippolytus, is to be found in
part IV of the *Félicia* mentioned above. There is
another similar plate in chap. XXI, not without charm.
Doris, in Epigram II of Sosipater(b) vol. I. of the
Analecta veterum Poetarum Graecorum, of Brunck (c)
(p. 504), seems also to have made a trial of this figure:

"When I stretched Doris with the rosy buttocks on
the bed, I felt immortal in my youthful vigor; for she
clipped me round the middle with her strong legs, and
unswervingly rode out the long course of Love."

Doris did not bestride him; the expression, "When I
stretched" shows this; she was lying on her back, and
with her feet lifted up clasped her rider.

But again the feet of the woman lying on her back
may also be held up by others. In this way Aloisio
enjoyed Tullia with the help of Fabrizio, in *Dialogue
VI*, of Luisa Sigea, where Tullia expresses herself as
follows:

"Aloisio and Fabrizio come running towards me.
"Lift up your legs," says Aloisio to me, threatening me
with his cutlass. I lifted them up. Then down he lies
on my bosom, and plunges his cutlass in my ever-open
wound. Fabrizio raised my two legs in the air, and
slipping a hand under each of my hams, moves my
loins for me without any trouble on my part. What a
singlar and pleasant mode of making you move! I

(b) Sosipater (fl 300 BC), a Greek comic poet.
(c) Richard Francois Philippe Brunck (1729-1803). He
collected all the known poems and fragments of otherwise
unpublished Greek poets. These also appear in his edition
of the Anthologia Graeca sive Poetarum Graecorum.

declared I was on fire, but before I could end my
sentence, the overflowing foam of Venus quenched the
fire." (10).

So too was it with feet in air, whether of her own
accord or seconded by another, that Leda gave herself, with her husband's consent, to the doctors who
had been called in, as Martial describes the scene:

"To her old spouse Leda had declared herself to be
hysterical, and complains she must needs be swived;
yet with tears and groans avers she will not buy health
at such a price, and swears she had rather die. The
husband beseeches her to live, not to die in her youth
and beauty; and permits others to do what he cannot
effect himself. Straightway the doctors arrive, the matrons retire; and up go the wife's legs in air; oh!
medicine grave and stern!" (XI, 71.)

Face downwards to her the man may do the woman's business, while she is half reclining, either obliquely in bed, or on a chair, or lying sideways.

The latter position is recommended by Ovid to the
woman with rounded thighs and faultless figure:

"She that has young rounded thigh and flawless
bosom, should ever lie reclined sideways on the
couch." (11)(*Art of Love*, III, 781-82).

---

(10) This method was not unknown at the time of Aristophanes, as we see from the following passage of the *Peace*:
"So that you may straightway, lifting up the girl's legs,
accomplish high in air the mysteries." (889-90).
And in the *Birds* he says:
"For you, girl, his first messenger, why! I will lift up your
legs and will in between your thighs." (1253-4).
(11) Readers will find another figure given in some of the
books:
"The man should be standing, while the woman reclines
sideways on the bed."

Copulation face to face with the woman sitting obliquely is described by Luisa Sigea with her usual elegance and vivacity:

"Caviceo came on, blithe and joyous" (it is Olympia speaking). "He despoils me of my chemise, and his libertine hand touches my parts. He tells me to sit down again as I was seated before, and places a chair under either foot in such a way that my legs were lifted high in air, and the gate of my garden was wide open to the assaults I was expecting. He then slides his right hand under my buttocks and draws me a little closer to him. With his left he supported the weight of his spear. Then he laid himself down on me ... put his battering-ram to my gate, inserted the head of his member into the outermost fissure, opening the lips of it with his fingers. But there he was stopped, and for a while made no further attack. 'Octavia sweetest,' he says, 'clasp me tightly, raise your right thigh and rest it on my side.—I do not know what you want,' I said. Hearing this he lifted my thigh with his own hand, and guided it around his loin, as he wished; finally he forced his mentula into the target of Venus. In the beginning he pushes in with gentle blows, then quicker, and at last with such force I could not doubt that I was in great danger. His member was hard as horn, and he forced it in so cruelly. I cried out, 'You will tear me to pieces!' He stopped a moment from his work. 'I implore you to be quiet my dear,' he said, 'it can only be done this way; endure it without flinching.' Again his hand slid under my buttocks, drawing me nearer, for I had made a feint to draw back, and without more delay plied me with such fast and furious blows that I was near fainting away. With a violent effort he forced his spear right in, and the point fixed itself in the depths of the wound. I cry out ... Caviceo spurted out his venereal exudation, and I felt drenched by a burning rain ... Just as Caviceo slackened, I experienced a sort of voluptuous itch as though I were making water; involuntarily I draw my buttocks back a little, and in an instant I felt with supreme pleasure something flowing from me which tickled me deliciously. My eyes sparkled, my breath came thick, my face was on fire, and I felt my whole body melting. 'Ah! ah! ah! my Caviceo, I shall faint away,' I cried; 'hold my soul—it is escaping from my body.'" (*Dialogue* V).'

Finally the conjunction with the woman lying on her side, particularly on her right side, is deemed by Ovid the most simple, calling for the least effort:

"A thousand modes of Love are there; the simplest and least laborious of all is when the woman lies reclined on her right side." (*Art of Love*, III, 787-88).

Above all, this position is the most convenient for tall women:

"Let her press the bed with her knees, with the neck slightly bowed, she whose chief beauty is her long shapely flank." (*Art of Love*, III, 779-80).

It seems that the Phyllis of Martial allowed herself to be done in that way:

"Two arrived in the morning, who wanted to lie with Phyllis, and each was fain to be first to hold her naked body in his arms; Phyllis promised to satisfy them both together, and she did it; one lifted her leg, the other her tunic." (X, 81).

She was lying on her side; the swiver lifted her leg; the pederast her tunic.

We now come to the manner in which the man
lying on his back has connection with the woman face
downwards. The parts are interchanged; the woman
plays the rider and the man the horse. This figure was
called the Horse of Hector.

Martial says:

"Behind the doors the Phrygian slaves would be
masturbating, every time Andromache mounted her
Hector horse-fashion." (X, 104).

Ovid, however, with much sagacity denies that this
posture could have pleased Andromache; her figure
was too tall, for this to have been agreeable or even
possible for her. It is for little women, that it is
pleasant to be thus placed:

"A little woman may very well get astride on her
horse; but tall and majestic as she was, the Theban
bride never mounted the Hectorean horse." (*Art of
Love*, III, 777-78).

It is no business of ours to decide the question.

At any rate Sempronia takes this posture with Crisogono.

"He could wait no longer: 'Are you undressed,' said
Crisogono. 'Now, my Sempronia, take the position
which gives me so much pleasure, you know which.'
He stretches himself down on his back, she gets upon
him astride, with her face towards him, and with her
own hand guides his burning arrow between her
thighs." (Luisa Sigea, *Dialogue* VII) (d).

(d) Dialogue VII was not included in the original work,
but was added in 1678. It is unknown whether Chorier was
the author of this dialogue—but Dialogue VII is set in
Italy, while the other six take place in Spain. There is now
no complete version of Dialogue VII, but only discon-
nected fragments.

This is the same attitude, which in Horace is imposed by the slave upon the little harlot, who:
" ... naked in the light of the lantern, plied with wanton wiles and moving buttocks the horse beneath her." (*Sat.* II. vii, 47-50) (e).

As to the matron spoken of in verse 64 of the same satire as "never having sinned *above*," no doubt this posture did not suit her. Women have not all the same taste.

Evidently, it was as little to the taste of the girl whom Xanthias in Aristophanes' *Wasps* (501-02) asked to ride him; for she asks him indignantly, and playing on the double meaning of the word (Hippias (f) and *hippos*, a horse), if he was for re-establishing Hippias' tyranny:

"Irritated she asked me if I wanted to revive the tyranny of Hippias."

Again in his *Lysistrata* (677) this master of wanton wit points to the same thing, declaring the female sex to be very good at riding and fond of driving:

"Woman loves to get on horseback and to stick there."

Aristophanes mocks similarly those, of whom he says, in verse 60 of the same play, that:
"They are aboard their barks."
"They are mounted on their chargers."
for *keles* signifies both a ship and a horse. Plango in

(e) Quintius Horatius Flaccus (65-8 BC,) one of the greatest Roman poets; published several books of *Odes* (Carmina), *Satires* (some of which are called also Sermones and Epistulae) and *Epodes*.
(f) Hippias, a son of Peisistratus—Tyrant (that is, not despot, but merely 'ruler by unconstitutional means') of Athens. Hippias succeeded his father but was forced into exile in 510 BC.

Asclepiades' Epigram XXIX (g) (Brunck's *Analecta*,
vol. I, p. 217) affects the same figure:

"When she vanquished the ardent Philaenis in
horsemanship, while her Hesperian coursers foamed
under her reins."

Yet more expert in this kind of amorous riding than
Philaenis herself, this ardent votary of pleasure thanks
Venus in this epigram, that she has been able so to
exhaust certain Hesperian gallants, whom she had
mounted, that they had left her with wanton members
all drooping, and feeling no desire left in them. To
bestride men was also the favorite pastime of Lysi-
dice, who was never tired in the service of Venus, of
whom the following epigram of Asclepiades treats:

"Many a horse has she ridden beneath her, yet
never galled her thigh with all her nimble movements."

Courtesans consecrated to Venus a whip, a bit, a
spur, in order to signify, that with their clients they
liked best to pose themselves in that way, and that
they preferred riding themselves to being ridden,—
nothing more.

It is the same when in Apuleius, (h) Fotis satiated
her Lucius with the pleasures of the undulating Venus:

"Saying this she leaped upon the couch and seated
upon me, plying her hips, vibrating her lithe spine
lasciviously, she satiated me with the delights of the
undulating Venus, till both of us exhausted, powerless

(g) Asclepiades of Samos; lived in the early 3rd Century,
BC; wrote 39 epigrams, most of which were erotic.
(h) Lucius Apuleius, born around 125 AD in Numidia.
Best known for his *Metamorphoses*, which later admirers
came to call, *The Golden Ass*.

and with useless limbs, sunk down, exhaling our souls
in mutual embraces." (*Metamorph.*, II, 17).

The next figure,—the man lying supine and the
woman turning her back to him, is executed by Rangoni with Ottavia, under the direction of Tullia:

Rangoni. Look how stiff I stand! But I want to try
the bliss in a new way.

Tullia. In a new way? No! I swear by my wanton
soul you shall not. You shall not take a new way.

Rangoni. It was a slip of the tongue; I meant to say
a new posture.

Tullia. And what sort of one? I have an idea ...
what they call the Horse of Hector. Lie down on your
back, Rangoni; let your splendid spear stand firm to
the enemy, who is to be pierced. Well done!

Ottavia. What must I do, Tullia?

Tullia. Clip Rangoni between your thighs, mounting
him a-straddle. His cutlass as he lies should meet your
sheath poised over it. Why! you've taken the position
admirably. Excellent!

Rangoni. Oh! what a back, worthy of Venus! Oh!
the ivory loins! Oh! the arousing buttocks!

Tullia. No naughty words! He who praises the
buttocks, slanders the vulva! You know better, Ottavia! Her greedy vulva has swallowed your bristling
member whole, Rangoni.

Ottavia. Quick, Rangoni, it is coming! ... quick,
quick, help me!

Rangoni. I am coming, Ottavia,—I am come! Are
you?—Are you, darling!

Tullia. Well? Are you so quickly finished, you two?
(Luisa Sigea, *Dialogue* VI).

The rituals of the buttocks (12), to which Eumolpus

---

(12) Pygiacic mysteries from *Pyge*—Buttock.

in Petronius (i) (*Satyricon*, ch. 140) invites a young
girl, refer to the position where the man lies on his
back, with the woman upon him, her back turned towards him.

"Eumolpus did not hesitate to invite the young girl
to the rituals of the buttocks, but begged of her to seat
herself upon the uprightness recommended to her
(that being himself, to whose goodness and uprightness the mother had recommended her daughter), and
ordered Corax to get on his stomach under the bed on
which he lay, so that with his hands pressed against
the floor, he might, with the movement of his loins,
assist those of his master. Corax obeyed, beginning
with slow undulations responding to those of the
young girl. When the crisis was approaching, Eumolpus exhorted Corax with a loud voice to quicken up
his movements. Thus placed between his servant and
his mistress, the old man took his pleasure as in a
swing."

Would it be surprising, if in these posterior mysteries, Eumolpus' member had perchance gone wrong,
and taken by mistake one orifice for the other?

You will find this figure represented in a copper-
plate engraving in the very elegant book of d'Hancarville, *Monuments du culte secret des dames romaines*,
ch. XXV, and you will be glad to know the note, with
which the learned annotator accompanies the same.

"This attitude is to the taste of many men, and even

(i) *The Satycrion* (properly, *Satirae*) of Petronius is
mostly lost. Only fragments of Book 15 and 16 remain of
the original 20 (probably) books. The author may be the
Gaius Petronius, *arbiter elegantiae*, mentioned by Tacitus
(*Annals*, XVI, 18-19) whom Nero forced to commit suicide in 66 AD. Or, he may be the Titus Petronius Arbiter
mentioned by Pliny the Elder and Plutarch.

the ladies find an increase of pleasure in practising it.
It is supposed, that Priapus penetrates farther in, and
that the fair one by her movements procures for
herself a more voluptuous delight and a more abundant libation."

Is it possible for the man, conveniently, to manage
the business while turning his back to the woman
lying on her back? Experts must decide. Luisa Sigea
says with good common sense:

"There are many postures it is impossible to execute, even supposing the joints and loins of the candi-
dates for the sacred joys of Venus more flexible than
can be believed. By dint of pondering and reflection
more ideas occur to the fancy than it is practicable to
realise. Nothing is inconceivable to the longings of an
unbridled will; nothing difficult to a furious and unre-
gulated imagination. Love will find out a way; and an
ardent fancy level mountains. Only the body is unable
to comply with everything the mind, good or bad,
suggests." (*Dialogue* VI.)

In another work of d'Hancarville's, *Monuments de
la vie privée des douze Césars*, plate XXVII, you find
represented men seated and copulating with women,
who are facing them; plate XV, in the same book
presents to your curiosity a man sitting and working a
woman, who turns her back on him. Augustus is
seated: he is attacking backwards, with true imperial
audacity, Terentia (13), the wife of Maecenas, after

_____
(13) Dio Cassius (k) (LIV, 19): "He was so fond of her,
that one day he matched her against Livia, as to which of
them was the most beautiful." It was no bad idea to
engage them in such a match, but think you he suffered
them to fight this out in any costume but that in which the
three Goddesses presented themselves before the dazed
eyes of Paris?

drawing her on to his lap; Maecenas is present, asleep
—asleep of course only for the Emperor. You may see
a similar posture in the *Contes et Nouvelles en vers* by
Jean de la Fontaine (j); it is on the plate appended to
the tale, called *Le Tableau*, p. 223, vol. II, Amsterdam,
1762.

Nothing is more frequent than conjunction while
standing, the woman with her face to the man; it is
indeed very easy to do it that way in any place, as you
have only to lift up the fair one's petticoats, and out
with your weapon; it is, therefore, the best manner for
those who have to make instantaneous use of an
opportunity, when it is important to be sharp about it,
as may happen, when you take your pleasure in secret.
Thus Priapus complains of the wives and daughters of
his neighbors, who came incessantly to him burning
with ticklish desires.

"Cut off my genital member, which every night and
all night long my neighbors' wives and daughters, forever and forever in heat, more wanton than sparrows
in springtide, tire to death,—or I shall burst! ..."
(*Priapeia*, XXVI).

I remember a medical man of our time, one of the
most celebrated professors (I had nearly uttered his
name), who to emphasize this, called his daughter, and

_____

(j) Jean de la Fontaine (1621-95), a French author of tales
and fables.
(k) Cassius Dio Cocceianus (ca. 150-225) was born at
Bithynia, the grandson of Dio Chrysostomus (Golden
Mouth) Cocceius, a famed essayist. Cassius Dio (or, as he
is usually called, Dio Cassius) was twice consul and is best
known for his extensive history of Rome, much of which is
lost.

pointing to the blushing girl, while his hearers could
not help smiling said: "This girl I fabricated standing."
A representation of this position is to be found in the
Monuments de la vie privée des douze Césars, pl.
XLVI, and another in the *Monuments du culte secret
des dames romaines*, pl. XIII.

But further, a man may join himself to a woman
standing face to face by supporting her in such a way,
that her whole body is lifted up, her thighs resting on
the man's hips, or else by lifting up the lower part of
her body, whilst the upper part is resting on a couch.
Will you feast your eyes with a representation of this
not ungraceful position? If so you will not omit to look
at plate XXIV of the *Monuments du culte secret des
dames romaines*, and plate XL of the *Monuments de
la vie privée des douze Césars*; Ovid, if I am not
mistaken, had his eyes on one or the other of these
figures:

"Milanion was supporting Atalanta's legs on his
shoulders; if they are fine legs this is how they should
be held." (*Art of Love*, III, 775-776).

The former of these modes is no doubt that described by Luisa Sigea, Past Mistress of these naught-
inesses, and with a vivacity, a grace, and elegance that
leaves nothing to be desired:

"La Tour came forward instantly ... I had thrown
myself on the foot of the bed"—(Tullia is speaking)—
"I was naked; his member was erect. Without more
ado he grasps in either hand one of my breasts, and
brandishing his hard and inflamed lance between my
thighs, exclaims 'Look Madam, how this weapon is
darting at you, not to kill you, but to give you the
greatest possible pleasure. Pray, guide this blind ap-

plicant into the dark recess, so that it may not miss its destination; I will not remove my hands from where they are, I would not deprive them of the bliss they enjoy.' I do as he wishes, I introduce myself the flaming dart into the burning centre; he feels it, drives in, pushes home ... After one or two strokes I felt myself melting away with incredible titillation, and my knees all but gave way. 'Stop,' I cried—'stop my soul, it is escaping!' 'I know,' he replied laughing, 'from where. No doubt your soul wants to escape through this lower orifice, of which I have possession; but I keep it well stoppered.' Whilst speaking he endeavored, by holding his breath, still further to increase the already enormous size of his swollen member. 'I am going to thrust back your escaping soul,' he added, poking me more and more violently. His sword pierced yet deeper into the quick. Redoubling his delicious blows, he filled me with transports of pleasure,—working so forcefully that, albeit he could not get his whole body into me, he impregnated me with all his passion, all his lascivious desires, his very thoughts, his whole delirious soul, by his voluptuous embraces. At last, feeling the approach of the ecstasy and the boiling over of the liquid, he slips his hands under my buttocks, and lifts me up bodily. I do my part; I twine my arms closely round his form, my thighs and legs being at the same time intertwisted and entangled with his, so that I found myself suspended on his neck in the air, lifted clean off the ground; I was thus hanging, as it were, fixed on a peg. I had not the patience to wait for him, as he was going on, and again I swooned with pleasure. In the most violent raptures I could not help crying out—'I feel all ... I feel all the delights of Juno lying with Jupiter. I

am in heaven.' At this moment, La Tour, pushed by
Venus and Cupid to the acme of voluptuousness,
poured a plenteous flood of his well into the genial
hold, burning like fire. The creeper does not cling
more closely round the walnut tree than I held fast to
La Tour with my arms and legs." (*Dialogue* VI).

As to the last manner by means of which copulation
may be achieved, the man standing with the woman
half-lifted up, Conrad, practises it with slight modifi-
cations.

(Tullia speaking): "He opened my thighs—I do not
dislike Conrad, though I am not particularly partial to
him. I neither consented, nor refused. As to him, he
fancied a novel posture, and not at all a bad one. I
was lying on my back; he raised my right thigh on his
shoulder, and in this position he transfixed me, while I
was awaiting the event, without greatly desiring it. He
had at the same time extended my left thigh along his
right thigh. His tool plunged in to the root, he began
to push and poke, quicker and quicker. What need to
say more? Picture the conclusion for yourself." (*Dialogue* VI).

Last of all, a man can get into a woman turning her
back to him after the manner of the quadrupeds, who
can have no connection with their females otherwise
than by mounting upon them from behind (14). Some

---

(14) Pliny (l) has treated this at great length in his
Natural History (Book X, 83).
(l) Gaius Plinius Secundus (23-79), Roman author,
known as Pliny the Elder to distinguish him from his
nephew, Gaius Plinius Caecilius Secundus (62-c.114)
(who is obviously known as Pliny the Younger). Pliny the
Elder wrote a *Natural History* in 37 books—none of which
has been lost—which is essentially an encyclopedia of the
knowledge of the ancient world—though it is full of
numerous mistakes and is marred by hasty research.

authorities have held that a woman conceives easier
while on all fours. Lucretius (m) says:

" ... Women are said to conceive more readily
when down after the manner of beasts, as the organs
can absorb the seed best so, when the bosom is
depressed and the loins lifted." (*Of the Nature of
Things*, IV, 1257-60).

Also Luisa Sigea:

"Some people pretend that the fashion to make love
indicated by Nature is that one where the woman
offers herself for copulation after the manner of the
animals, bent down with the hips raised; the virile
ploughshare penetrates thus more conveniently into
the female furrow, and the seminal flow waters the
field of love ... The doctors, however, are against this
posture; they say it is incompatible with the conforma-
tion of the parts destined for generation." (*Dialogue*
VI.)

However this may be, it happens frequently, that
women cannot be managed in any other way. Given
an obese man and a woman likewise obese or with
child, how are they to do the thing otherwise? This is
the reason why, so they say, Augustus having married
Livia Drusilla, divorced wife of Tiberius Nero and
already six months gone in pregnancy, had connection
with her after the manner of animals. Plate VII of the
Monuments de la vie privée des douze Césars will
give you an idea of the posture assumed by both of
them. But why should we not give you the annotations
whereby the learned editor has elucidated the plate?

(m) Titus Lucrettius Carus (c. 96-55) a Roman who wrote
De Rerum Natura (Of The Nature of Things) which is the
chief source of our knowledge of Epicurean philosophy.

Here they are:

"This Drusilla was the famous Livia, the wife of
Tiberius Nero, who had been one of Anthony's
friends. Augustus fell violently in love with her, and
Tiberius gave her up to him, although she was at the
time six months with child. A good many jokes were
made about the eagerness of the Emperor, and one
day, while they were all at table, and Livia was
reclining by Augustus, one of those naked children,
whom matrons used to educate for their pleasures,
going up to Livia said: 'What are you doing here?
younder is your husband,' pointing to Nero, 'there he
is.' (15). Soon afterwards Livia was confined, and the
Romans said openly, that lucky people get children
three months after being married, which passed into a
proverb. One historian says that Augustus was obliged
to caress his wife 'after the manner of beasts' on
account of her pregnancy, and it was to this luxurious
attitude that the cameo of Apollonius, the celebrated
gem-cutter of the time of Augustus, makes allusion.
True that the state in which Livia was may have made
this posture necessary: but it seems that it was at all
times to the taste of the Ancients, either because they
considered this attitude favourable for procreation, as
Lucretius maintains, or because they found it to be a
refinement of voluptuousness. The most extraordinary
and least natural postures have always appeared to
rakes as enhancing the pleasure of the conjunction.
But it must be admitted that imagination still outruns
actual possibilities."

A singular reason for the necessity of encountering a

----

(15) Compare Dio Cassius (bk. XLVIII, 44).

woman backwards is given by Luisa Sigea, with her
usual sagacity:

"For pleasure, one likes a vulva which is not placed
too far back, so as to be entirely hidden by the thighs;
it should not be more than nine or ten inches from the
navel. With the greater number of girls the pubis goes
so far down, that it may easily be taken as the other
way of pleasure. With such coition is difficult. Theo-
dora Aspilqueta could not be deflowered, till she
placed herself prone on her stomach, with her knees
drawn up to her sides. Vainly had her husband tried
to manage her, while lying on her back, he only lost
his oil." (*Dialogue* VII).

Ovid recommends this way with women who begin
to be wrinkled:

"Likewise you, whose stomach Lucina has marked
with wrinkles, mount from behind, like the flying
Parthian with his steed." (*Art of love*, III, 785-86).

The same advice also seems to be given by him a
little before:

"Let them be seen from behind whose backs are
sightly." (III, 774).

But besides necessity, it is a fact that women are
worked in this way out of mere caprice, variety offering the greatest pleasure. It is simply for this reason
that Tullia suffers Fabrizio to do her that way, in
Luisa Sigea:

"As Aloisio got up" (Tullia speaks) "Fabrizio makes
ready for another attack. His member is swollen up,
red and threatening. 'I beg of you Madam,' he says,
'turn over on your face.' I did as he wished. When he
saw my buttocks, whiter than ivory and snow, 'How
beautiful you are!' he cried. 'But raise yourself on your

knees, and bend your head down.' I bow my head and
bosom, and lift my buttocks. He thrust his swift-mov-
ing and fiery dart to the bottom of my vulva, and took
one of my nipples in either hand. Then he began to
work in and out, and soon sent a sweet rivulet into the
cavity of Venus. I also felt unspeakable delight, and
had nearly fainted with lust. A surprising quantity of
seed secreted by Fabrizio's loins filled and delighted
me; a similar flow of my own exhausted my forces. In
that single assault I lost more vigor than in the three
preceding ones." (*Dialogue* VI) (16).

This copulation from the back is practicable in
another very pleasant fashion, an excellent reproduc-
tion of which can be seen in the *Monument du culte
secret des dames romaines*, plate XXVIII. A woman is
represented with her hands placed on the ground,
while the lower part of the body is lifted up and
suspended by cords; she is turning her back to the
man who stands. This seems to be much the same
position as was taken up by the wife of the artisan
Apuleius speaks of in his *Metamorphoses* (book IX, 7),
whom "bending over her, the lover planed with his
adze, while she leaned forward over a cask." An
engraving showing this ingenious attitude is appended
to the story of *The Tub* in the *Contes et Nouvelles en
vers* of Jean de La Fontaine, (vol. II, p. 215).

----

(16) The thing itself is very old; Aristophanes alludes to it
in the *peace:*
"To wrestle on the ground, to stand on all fours." (896).
And in the *Lysistrata:*
"I will not squat down like a lioness carved on a knife-han-
dle." (231).

OF PEDICATION

CHAPTER TWO

OF PEDICATION

So much for copulation in the usual way. We will
now discuss another mode of pleasure,—that due to
introduction of the member into the anus. A man who
exercises his member in the anus, be it of a man or a
woman, pedicates; he is called a pederast, a pedicon,
drawk (17), and the other party, who allows himself to
be invaded in that way, is called the patient, cinaedus,
catamite (18), minion, effeminate; if adult or worn out,
he is named exolete. The masculine pleasure so called

---

(17) *Drawk*, from the Greek, *drao*, I work, execute; *drawk*
an English corruption from *draucus* for *dravicus*, as *cautus*
for *cavitus*, *lautus* for *lavitus*.

(18) Catamite, according to Festus (a), is the same thing
as Ganymede, the minion of Jupiter; the Latins, by similar corruption of words, pronounced *Proserpina* for *Perse-
phone*, *Aesculapius* for *Asclepios*, *Carthago* for *Carchedo*,
Pollux for *Polydeukes*, *Sybilla* for *Siobule*, *masturbare* for
manu stuprare.

(a) Sextus Pompeius Festus (2nd century AD) Roman
author of a dictionary, *De Verborum Significatione*, only
half of which has survived.

because women allowed themselves much more rarely
to be pedicated than men is appreciated equally by
the active party, the pedicon, as by the passive party,
the patient. The pleasure of the pedicon is easy to
understand, as the enjoyment of the virile member
consists in the intensity of the friction; the pleasure
felt by the patient by the introduction of the member
in his entrails is more difficult to make out,—at least
for my feeble intelligence, for such practices are quite
strange to me. Do not believe, however, that the
pleasure of the patient is only secondary, nor yet that
he prostitutes himself only in order to do the same
afterwards himself, nor that he remedies in this way
the sluggishness of his own member by the vigorous
working of another man's nerve causing a pleasurable
titillation of the posterior, analogous to that which
Antonius Panormitanus (b) (*Hermaphroditus*, I, 20)
tells us may be produced by inserting the fingers in
the anus (19), or still better, by beating the same
locality with rods, according to Luisa Sigea:

"Amongst the men of our acquaintance, I have

(b) Antonius Panormitanus has been treated above, and it
is his *Hermaphroditus* which caused the creation of this
work by Forberg. He is actually Antonio Beccadelli
(1393-1471) of a noble family from Bologna, but, being
born at Palermo (in Latin, Panormus), he took the name
Antonius Panormitanus (Antonio of Palermo).
(19) Thus Oenothea, to excite the lad's feeble nerve,
pushes a leather mentula into Encolpius anus (Petronius,
138): "Oenothea fetches a leather contrivance; this she first
oiled and sprinkled with pepper and crushed nettle-seeds,
and then proceeded to push little by little up my anus."
We shall have to speak in chapter VI, of another use of
these leather tools.

heard the Marquis Alfonso say that rods act as spurs
to the amorous battle; without them he would be
sluggish and impotent. He has his buttocks flogged
with rods vigorously, his wife being present lying
ready on the bed. During the flagellation his tool
begins to stiffen, and the more violent the strokes are,
the stronger is the tension. When he feels himself in
proper condition, he precipitates himself upon his
wife, works her with rapid movement, and inundates
her with the heavenly gifts of Venus, and wins all the
delights a man may find in love." (20) (*Dialogue* V).

What else was it but this that so stirred Rousseau
(c), the precocious genius of Geneva, and his boyish
member, and brought such ideas into his head, when
on one occasion Mlle. Lambercier, cracking the whip
upon the buttocks of the child, inflicted that punishment, which ne afterwards was longing for all the rest
of his life? Hear him relate the circumstance himself
in his merry way and with his habitual charm of style,
in the first book of the *Confessions*; we only omit
small matters, added by the immortal author for the
amplification of the narrative:

"As Mlle. Lambercier had for us the affection of a
mother, so she had the authority of one, and she
carried the latter so far as to inflict upon us the
punishment of children when we had deserved it. For

(20) According to the author of the *Gynaeology* (German
edition, vol. III, p. 392) there are to be found at this day
in the London brotheis women who make it their business
to flagellate customers who desire it.
(c) Jean-Jacques Rousseau (1712-1778), French philosopher and writer who had a big influence on the political
thought and art of the Romantic Age.

a long time she only used threats, and such a threat of
a novel punishment seemed very dreadful to me; but
after the execution I found the experience less terrible
than the expectation, and the oddest thing was, that
the punishment made me more partial to her, who had
inflicted it, than I had been previously. I stood in fact
in need of all this affection for her and of all my
natural mildness, in order to hold back from provok-
ing the same punishment by acting so as to deserve it,
for I had found in the pain, and even in the shame, a
mixed feeling, in which sensuality predominated, and
which left me with more desire than apprehension of
experiencing the same treatment over again from the
same hand. Who would believe that this chastisement
of a child eight years old by the hand of a maiden of
thirty should have influenced my tastes, my longings,
my passions, for the remainder of my life? Tormented
by I know not what, my eye feasted ardently upon
good-looking females; they constantly came into my
mind doing to me as Mlle. Lambercier had done.
Imagining only what I had experienced, my desires
did not pass beyond the sort of voluptuous feeling I
had known already. In my foolish fancies, in my erotic
fury, in the extravagant acts to which they incited me
sometimes, I borrowed in imagination the help of
the other sex, without ever dreaming it was good for
any other use than that which I wanted to make of it.
When in the course of time I had grown up to
manhood, my old taste of childhood associated itself
so much with the other, that I never could divert the
desires which fired my senses; and this absurdity,
joined to my natural timidity, made me always any-

thing but enterprising with women, as I dared not say
all or could not do all I wanted; the sort of enjoyment,
of which the other was for me but the last stage, could
neither be initiated by the one who longed for it, nor
guessed at by the other who might have granted it.
Thus I have passed through life coveting, yet not
daring to tell the persons I loved most what it was I
coveted. Never bold enough to declare my inclination,
I amused it at least by ideas in connection with it. One
may judge what such avowals must have cost me,
considering that all through my life, seized in the
presence of those I loved by the fury of a passion
which bereft me of voice, hearing and sense, and
made me tremble all over convulsively, I never could
venture to tell them my folly, and ask them to add the
one familiarity which I wanted to the other ones. I
only got to it once in my childhood, with another child
of my age, and the proposal came from her."

However to return to our proper subject, from
which we have strayed. If pleasure felt by the passive
party cannot be conceived to be of a kind, which
through the anus is communicated to the mentula, we
must come to the conclusion that the patient exper-
iences in the anus the same kind of irritation which
the other party feels in his genital parts; that, therefore, the patient feels in that place a real pleasure
unknown to those who have not tried it (21). Martial
at any rate speaks out without any circumlocution of

---

(21) In order to appease the ardors of the anus, the
Siphnians (Siphnos, one of the Cyclades) were in the habit
of introducing a finger up the anus. The Greeks called this
proceeding to *siphnianize*. Suidas: *Siphnianize*,—to finger
the posterior.

this rut of the anus:

"Of his anus, split to the navel, not a vestige is left
to Carinus; for all that he is in rut to the very navel
Oh! the scurvy lot of the wretch! Bottom he has none,
—but he *will* be a cinede." (VI, 37).

An ardor of this strange sort even affected Tullia, as
she confesses herself in the pages of Luisa Sigea:

"Seeing resistance was in vain, I yielded to the
madmen. Aloisio bends forward over my buttocks,
brings his javelin to the backdoor, knocks, pushes,
finally with a mighty effort bursts in. I gave a groan.
Instantly he withdraws his weapon from the wound,
plunges it in the vulva and spurts a flood of semen
into the wanton furrow of my womb. When it was
over Fabrizio attacks me in the same fashion. With one
rapid thrust he introduced his spear, and in less than
no time made it disappear in my entrails; for a little
time he plays at come and go, and scarcely credible as
it may sound, I found myself invaded by a prurient
fury to such an extent that I have no doubt, that I
should get accustomed to it very well, if l chose."
(*Dialogue* VI).

Coelius Rhodiginus confirms this pruriency of the
anus in chap. 10 of the XVth book of his *Lectiones
antiquae*.

"We know," he says, "that the minions experience a
very great pleasure in undergoing this shameful act."

And he gives a reason for it too, whether good or
bad the doctors may decide:

"With people whose seminal ducts are not in normal
condition, be it that those leading to the mentula are
paralysed, as is the case with eunuchs and the like, or

for any other reason, the seminal fluid flows back to its
source. If this fluid is very abundant with them, it
accumulates in great quantities, and then the part
where the secretion is accumulated longs for friction.
People thus situated like above everything to play the
part of patients."

Be this as it may, nothing is more certain than the
fact of such enjoyment on the part of the patient. So
highly did the Roman cinedes prize a stiff member
between their buttocks, that they could not see a big
mentula without their mouths watering; they were
ready to give their last penny to enjoy the favors of a
man extraordinarily gifted in that way.

Juvenal (d) *Satirae*, IX, 32-36):

"Destiny governs men; it influences the parts
which the toga covers. If your star pales, even the
most phenomonally long member will be of no use to
you, even though Virro should have seen you naked,
his lips drooling."

Martial (I, 97):

"He wants to know why I think he is a minion? We
bathe together; he never raises his eyes, but
gazes with devouring looks at the sodomites; and
cannot behold their members without his lips trembling."

And again (II, 51):

"Oftentimes you have no more than a single penny
in your box, and that penny more worn than your
anus, Hyllus; yet neither baker nor wine-shop will

_____
(d) Decimus Junius Juvenalis, born around 47 AD and
died after 127, probably in exile. Little is known of his life.
He left 16 satires, which are mostly a condemnation of the
corruption and licentiousness of 1st-century Rome.

have it, but some man who sports an enormous member. Your unfortunate belly must starve for your anus; while the latter devours, the former is famished."

It is therefore not astonishing that the public baths resounded with plaudits, when men with extraordinary members entered them.

Martial (IX, 34):

"If you hear clapping of hands in the bathing hall, Flaccus, you may be sure some handsome member is there."

Juvenal (VI, 373-374):

"Conspicuous from afar, and altogether outstanding, he enters the baths."

It was not without some art that the patients performed their functions. But their business was made up of these two chief requirements: depilation and knowing how to use the haunches.

Patients took care in the first place to remove the hair carefully from all parts of their body (22); from the lips, arms, chest, legs, the virile parts, and in particular from the altar of passive lust, the anus:

Martial (II, 62):

"Pluck out the hair from breast and legs and arms;

---

(22) Always, however, excepting the head, for they took great care of their head of hair.
Horace (*Ode* X, book IV, 3, To Ligurinus) says:
"When those curls are gone, that now descend to your shoulders . . ."
And (*Epode* XI, 23-28) where he states that nothing will take away his love for Lyciscus, save another love for a plump youth, tying up his long hair. In the same sense Martial speaks of *Capillati* (III, 58, line 31; II, 57, line 5), and of *Comati* (long haired) (XII, 98, line 4).

keep your member cropped and ringed with short
hair; all this, we know, you do for your mistress' sake,
Labienus. But for whom do you depilate your posteriors?"

And (IX, 28):

"While you, Chrestus, appear thus with your parts
all hairless, with a mentula like a vulture's neck, and a
head as shining as a prostitute's buttocks with never a
hair appearing on your leg, and with your pallid lips
all shorn and bare, you talk of Curius, Camillus,
Numa, Ancus, of all the hairy heroes we have ever
read of in history, and spout big words and threaten-
ings against theatres and the times. Let but some
big-limbed man come into sight, you call him with a
nod, and take him off . . ."

And he says (IX, 58):

"Nought is worse worn than Hedylus' rags, save one
thing only (he cannot deny it himself), his anus;—this
is worse worn than his rags."

In a similar way he has spoken before of the anus of
Hyllus as more worn by friction than a poor man's last
penny (II, 51), and Suetonius (*Life of Otho*, XII)
speaks similarly of the body of Otho, given to the
habits of a catamite, and Catullus (*Carm*. XXXIII, 7-8)
(e) reproaches the younger Vibennius: "You could not
sell your hairy buttocks for a doit."

For the same reason Galba requested Icelus to get
depilated before he was to take him aside. Suetonius,
Galba (XXII):

"He was very much given to sexual intercourse

_____

(e) Gaius Valerius Catullus (87-c54 BC) one of the
greatest lyric poets. Many of his poems are addressed to
Lesbia, who was probably the notorious Clodia (see below).

between men, and he preferred strong, mature men. It
is said that when Icelus, one of his old bedfellows,
came to Spain, to inform him of Nero's death, he, not
content with kissing him closely before everyone present, asked him to get at once depilated, and then took
him aside."

Moreover even those depilated their anus, who by
dint of a rough head of hair and a bristly beard, tried
hard to simulate the gravity of the ancient Philosophers.

Martial (IX, 48):

"Democritus and Zeno and ambiguous Plato,—all
the sages whose portraits we see decked with bristling
hair,—you prate of; you might well be Pythagoras'
heir and successor; while from your own chin hangs
no less imposing a beard. But as a bearded man it is a
shame for you to receive a rigid member between
your smooth posteriors."

Juvenal (II, 8-13):

"Don't trust the face; for what street is not overflowing with offensive obscenities? You censure scandalous behavior, when you are the most notorious gutter
among the Socratic cinedes; shaggy legs and coarse
hair along the arms are assurance of a savage disposi-
tion, to be sure, but on your smooth anus the surgeon
cuts away the swollen piles, a grin on his face the
while."

Persius (f) (IV, 37, 38):

"Tell me, when you comb a scented beard upon
your cheeks, why does a shaven member stand forth
from your groin?"

This is why Martial (VI, 56) advised Charidemus to

(f) Aulus Persius Flaccus (34-62), Roman author of six
satires, which condemn the follies of his age and emphasize the ethics of stoicism.

get his buttocks depilated, so that he might be taken
for a patient rather than for a fellator:

"Because your thighs bristle with coarse hair, and
your chest is shaggy, you think, Charidemus, to leave
your words to posterity.

"Take my word, and pluck out the hairs all over
your body, and get it certified you depilate your
buttocks. What for? you ask. You know they tell many
tales about you; make them believe, Charidemus, that
you are acting the patient."

It was not patients only that had themselves depilated; men leading an idle, careless life followed the
same practice. (23)

"To be depilated, to have the hair dressed in tiers of
ringlets, to tipple to excess in the baths,—these practices prevail in the city; still they cannot be said to be
customary, for nothing of all this is exempt from
blame." (Quintilian (g), *Instit. orat.*, I, 6).

It is rather surprising that the same Quintilian,
whose bile is stirred by curled hair, has let it pass by
patiently, that women should bathe together with
men:

"If it is a sure sign of adultery for a woman to bathe

---

(23) To depilate one's armpits was, however considered as
being necessary to the cleanliness of the body: "One man
keeps himself tidy, another neglects himself more than is
right; one man depilates his legs, another does not depilate
even his armpits." (Seneca, *Letter* CXIV).

(g) Marcus Fabius Quintilianus (ca. 35 AD-97/100), born in
Spain, he opened a school of rhetoric in Rome (subsidised
by the state). He wrote *De Institutione Oratoria* which
tells much of the practice (and theory) of education.

with men, why it will be adultery to dine with young
friends of the male sex, to have a male friend. You
might as reasonably say a depilated body, a languid
gait, a womanish robe, are certain signs of effeminacy,
of want of virility; for such will seem to many to
reveal immorality of character." (*Ibid.*, V, 9).

Martial (II, 29) has also noticed, and not once only,
the habits of those men who practised feminine arts of
the toilette, and looked just as if they had come out of
a band-box:

"Rufus, see you that man there on the first benches
... whose oiled curls exhale the whole shop of Marce-
lianus, and whose polished arms shine without a hair
to be seen?"

Again, he says (V, 61):

" ... Who is this Crispulus, ... who has legs
undisfigured by a single hair?"

Even the great Caesar did not disdain this coquetry:
Suetonius (ch. 45):

"He took too much care of his appearance, to the
point of not only being trimmed and shaved, but even
of being depilated, for which things he was reproached."

This custom is connected with those Samnite
vases, filled with rosin and pitch to be heated for
depilation, and for softening the pitch, found amongst
the properties of Commodus, and which by the orders
of Pertinax were sold by public auction. Julius Capitolinus (h) speaks of them (*Pertinax*, VIII, 5-6). For
removing the hair there were used in fact either
tweezers or an unguent called dropax or psilothrum.

(h) Julius Capitolinus, a minor Roman historian who lived
in the early 4th century, AD

Martial mentions the use of the tweezers in the *Epigram* (IX, 28) quoted before; of dropax or psilothrum he speaks in Book III, 74:

"You depilate your face with psilothrum and your head with dropax."

And again (VI, 93):

"She revives her youth with psilothrum."

And (X, 65):

"You rub yourself every day with dropax."

The dropax or psilothrum was obtained by melting rosin in oil (Pliny, *Natural History*, XIV, 20):

"All rosin dissolves in oil, ... and I am ashamed to say, that the most honest use made of this mixture is to serve as a depilatory for men."

Aetius (i) also mentions it in Book III, ch. 190, of his *Opus Medicum*:

"The simplest dropax is the one called pitch-plaster. Dry pitch is diluted with oil; it is applied hot to the skin, which must first be cleanly shaved, under which circumstances it adheres closely. Before the plaster is quite cold, it is taken off, warmed again, and put on afresh; again it is removed before being cold, and this process is repeated several times."

Hence Juvenal's "Youthfulness by pitch," (VIII, 114), and

"The thighs neglected and dirty with tufts of hair" of Naevolus, to whom he says:

"Your skin has none of the gloss, that of old the well-smeared plaster of hot pitch gave it." (*Sat.* IX, 13-15).

What else does Martial mean when (III, 74) he

(i) Aetius (6th century AD), of Mesopotamia. A Byzantine physician at Constantinople.

speaks of "Gargilanus' nails,—that cannot be trimmed
with pitch?"

Persius (IV, 37-41) has, I presume, joined together
both modes of depilation:

"Tell me, when you comb a scented beard upon
your cheeks, why does a shaven member stand forth
from your groin? Though five strong men weed your
plantation and work your parboiled buttocks with the
hooked forceps, I tell you there is no plow will tame
that stubborn field!"

Her *forceps* is the same thing as *volsella* (tweezers);
while the "parboiled buttocks" would seem to refer
to the hot dropax. After the application of such
a plaster the skin could not but have a boiled look.

Ausonius (j) (*Epigr.* CXXXI.) alludes to this passage of Persius:

"The reason you smooth your groin with hot dropax
is that a skin soft and smooth entices the whores. But
that you pluck out the foliage from your boiled bottom, and polish up with pumice your battered Clazomenae, what means this,—if not that the vice of man
with man (*patientia morbum*) attacks you, and you are
a woman behind, a man in front."

The *Clazomenae* are without a doubt the man's
buttocks, limp and cracked, as those of patients will
be, as those of Carinus were, whom Martial (VI, 37)
blames for "his lacerated anus." Ausonius calls them so
from the Greek *klazo*, in Latin "frango" (I break), thus
playing with the name of a city. Gonzalvo the Corde-

(j) Decimus Magnus Ausonius (c310-c390), a scholar of
Bordeaux, tutor to Emperor Gratian (375-83). Author of
Mosella—which some consider a great poem—and many
Epigrams.

van makes a similar pun, when, desiring to pedicate,
he says, he wishes to go to Aversa; also when he
wishes to irrumate the mouth, he says: "I go to the
Orient," or when he is about to lick the vulva, in Latin
ligurire, "I go to Liguria." By calling the Clazomenae
hammered (battered) Ausonius means to imply that
they were as if polished with a hammer, by having
served as an anvil. It is as if my fellow-countrymen
were to say in joke of a bald man (in German *Kahl*),
"he scratches his polished *Kehl*. (k)" What could be
clearer or wittier? Forcellini is therefore wrong in
saying this passage of Ausonius has no sense. Other
editors have *inclusas* instead of *incusas*, indicating the
fissure which separates the buttocks, by the rotundi-
ties of which it is on both sides closed in. But in the
first place the Clazomenae may well be the buttocks,
they being cleft, though not indeed themselves a cleft;
in the second place, who could imagine this miserable
man depilated the cleft of the buttocks rather than the
buttocks themselves?

Some persons, by a refinement of luxury, employed
women to depilate them. Such women called themselves *ustriculae* (from *urere*, to burn), as they made
use of a sticky plaster of boiling dropax to burn the
hair on the legs and other parts of the body. Tertullian
(1) (*De Pallio*, 4), says: "So effeminate as to employ
ustriculae"; while Salmasius (m), commenting playful-

(k) *Kehl* is throat or gullet. I fail to discern the wit in this.
(l) Quintus Septimius Florens Tertullianus (c160-c230),
born at Carthage of a non-Christian family, he became one
of the earliest Christian writers.
(m) Claudius Salmasius (Claude Saumaise) (1588-1653),
Latin, Arabic scholar who replaced Joseph Scaliger at
Leiden.

ly on the passage (p. 284), declares: "Once upon a time
ustriculae served to depilate the legs; now they serve
to harass our minds." Augustus, who according to
Suetonius, "used to singe his legs with burning nut-
shells, to make the hair grow more silky," (*Augustus*,
68), no doubt made use of the nimble hands of these
ustriculae.

Women likewise resorted to depilation (24), looking

---

(24) The Greeks did not disdain this strange practice any
more than the Romans. Aristophanes, in the *Lysistrata* (v.
89). (n)
"My affair will be tidy with the couchgrass pluck'd off."
In the *Frogs* (515-16) he speaks of "dancing girls barely
arrived at puberty beginning to tear off the fur." In the
Ecclesiazusae (724) again there is mentioned "a *mons
Veneris* plucked clean." That the Greeks preferred a bare
pubis to a furred one, though we may be of a different
opinion, is apparent from another passage of Aristophanes,
in the *Lysistrata*, (v. 151-2) where a smooth pubis is
represented as a chief incitement to virile ardor:
"If we were to go naked with a smooth pubis, our
husbands' members would stand, and they would want to
have us."
As to old women, they likewise denuded their pubis of the
bristles in order to appear less decrepit. Martial, (X, 90):
"Ligella, do you pluck your old affair, and stir the ashes of
your burnt-out fire? Refinements such as those are for
young maidens; you are in error if you think that thing a
vulva that a man's member will no longer recognise."
The depilation of the vulva was also used as a punishment.
Aristophanes (*Thesmophoriazusae* 545-6):
The same punishment was inflicted upon adulterous women taken in the act; a black radish or a mullet was
introduced into her anus, which was then depilated, as
well as her pubis, with burning cinders. Aristophanes
(*Clouds*, 1079):
"What, must you suffer the empalement with the radish,

upon the fleece of the pubis as something disgusting. Martial:

"... Nor yet one of your mother's pots full of foul rosin, such as the women of the outer suburbs use to depilate themselves with." (XII, 32).

As men employed women to free them of hair, so women offered their pubis without shame to men for the same office. Pliny's bile rises at this (*Nat. Hist.*, VIII, 26-7).:

"Women are not afraid to show their pubis. It is but too true, nothing corrupts manners more than the art of the medical man."

The emperors themselves condescended to undertake this office for their concubines.

Suetonius (*Domitian*, 22):

"It was rumored, that he was fond of depilating his concubines himself, and would bathe amid a crowd of the most infamous prostitutes."

Lampridius (o), (*Heliogabalus*, 31):

"In his baths he was always together with the women, and he made their toilets with psilothrum: he

_____

and the hot cinders?"

Suidas, under the word *raphanis*: "Thus they treated adulteresses who had been caught in the act: they took black radishes and planted them in their anus, which they rubbed with hot cinders, after having torn out the hair."

(n) These references, in context, and the next few quotations suggest that the Greeks looked on a shaven pubis as a punishment—though young girls may have done this to appear as if they had not yet reached puberty, which may be what Martial has in mind in reference to Ligella.

(o) Aelius Lampridius, a minor Roman historian who lived in the early 4th century AD.

used psilothrum likewise for his beard, and, disgusting
to relate, the same which the women had just been
using. With his own hand he shaved off the fleece
from the virile part of his pedicons, and then shaved
his own beard."

What Lampridius finds so repugnant, is that the
emperor did not hesitate to use upon his beard the
same ointment, which the women had just been applying as a plaster upon the pubis, and which he used at
once and before the bad smell had evaporated.

But to return to our patients, they also were not in
want of illustrious lovers, who took care to depilate
them; an example of this we find in the emperor
Hadrian, according to Spartianus (p), who says (IV,
5):

"That he corrupted the freedmen of Trajan, made
the toilet of his minions, and often depilated them (q),
while he was attached to the Court, is generally
believed."

In what other way can we believe Hadrian to have
made the toilet of these minions, if not in the same
way in which Heliogabalus made the toilet of his
females, with psilothrum, particularly as it is added
that he depilated them frequently? We may take it for
granted that he used that ointment, or that he rubbed
their faces with moistened bread, either to improve

(p) Aelianus Spartianus, a minor Roman historian who
lived in the late 3rd century AD.
(q) The text is corrupt and there are variant readings for
"often depilated them." (1) "buried them" (which hardly
fits with the rest); (2) "prostituted himself to them," which
is possible. "Made the toilet of his minions," may also be
rendered "indulged his minions."

their skin or to hinder the beard growing too soon. Suetonius (*Otho*, 12):

"He shaved his face every day, and rubbed it with damp bread, a habit which he had contracted when the first down began to appear, so as to never have a beard."

Juvenal (II, 107), has aimed an arrow of the same sort at Otho:

"It surely is the duty of a mighty Captain ... to keep his skin right smooth ... and knead bread with his fingers to make a plaster for his face."

What wonder then if the women cherished similar artifices? Who can help thinking of the woman depicted with such marvellous art by Juvenal, from verse 460 to verse 472 of that Sixth Satire, to which Salmasius gave the epithet, of "divine"? "Her face is all puffy with bread crumbs, where the lips of the poor husband keep sticking," to such an extent, that one doubts:

" ... Whether her countenance, plastered and massaged with so many preparations, overlaid with poultices of boiled and moistened flour, should be called a face at all,—or a sore ... At last she peels her face, removes the outermost layers. For the first time she may be recognised for herself. Then she treats her skin with asses' milk, for which she drags about in her train a herd of asses,—and would take them with her, if she were exiled to the North Pole."

For painting the face it seems that a coating of chalk was used, as in the case of the pederast mentioned in Petronius, who perspired so violently in working vainly the groin of Encolpius:

"From his perspiring forehead flowed rivulets of

acacia juice, and in the wrinkles of his cheeks there
was such a mass of chalk that you might have believed
you saw a wall exposed to the wind and washed by
the rain." (*Satyricon*, 23).

But let us leave all these nasty preparations, before
we find ourselves stuck fast in them.

We have said that another branch of this business,
on the part of the patient, consists in *cevere*. A *patient
cevet*, who during the action wriggles and moves his
haunches up and down, so as to enjoy more pleasure
himself and give more pleasure to the pedicon. Wom-
en, doing the same in copulation, are said to *crissare*.
Martial (III, 95):

"Nay! you pedicate finely, Naevolus; you ply your
haunches right well."

Juvenal (II, 20-23):

" ... Virtue on their lips, they ply their buttocks—
'Shall I honor you, in the act of your haunch-wiggling,
Sextus?' says the infamous Varillus ..."

The same author (IX, 40):

"With calculated art moves his haunches."

Plautus (r), in the *Pseudolus* (III, sc. 2, 75):

"As soon as he cowers down, wriggle your buttocks
in time to him."

For this reason some authorities hold, I do not know
whether rightly or wrongly, the word *cinede* to come
from the fact that the wretches known by that name
are in the habit of *wriggling the private parts* (in
Greek, *kinein ta aidoia*). Undoubtedly the suppleness
of the thighs, the agility of the buttocks, are counted

(r) Titus Maccius Plautus (254-184 BC) Roman author of
comic plays—some of which served as models for later
playwrights, such as Shakespeare and Moliere.

amongst the particular talents of cinedes in Petronius
(23):

Enter a cinede reciting these verses:

"Hither, come hither, cinede wantons,—stretch the
foot and take your course, fly with soles in the air,
with supple thighs, and nimble buttocks, and libertine
hands,—all ye old, emasculated minions of Delos,
come!"

To this subject also refers Epigram XXXVI of the
Ist. Book of the *Hermaphroditus*, edited by us; which
consult, reader, if worth your while. (s) As he who
wriggles with his haunches does it to please somebody, people use the word *cevere* also to convey the
meaning of sycophancy or adulation. Thus in Persius
(I, 87): "*An Romule ceves?*" (What Romulus, you fawn
too?); in the same way *irrumate* is used in the sense of
an outrage, affront.

That women *can* be pedicated, exactly the same as
men, is indicated by nature; that they *have* consented,
is proved by numerous testimonies in Antiquity.—
Apuleius (*Metamorphosis*, III, 20):

"While we were thus bickering, a mutual passion
invaded our minds and excited our bodies; having
undressed entirely we revelled nakedly in sexual delights. I soon felt tired. Fotis with her affability thrust
her buttocks toward me to sodomize."

Martial (IX, 68):

(s) Since few of the readers will be able to consult the
Hermaphroditus—whether worth their while or not—I
include Epigram XXXVI. On the Pedicon, Matius Lupius:
Lupius, while pedicating an ignorant youth, said, "Come
on! Shake your butt, sweet youth." "All right," replied the
other, "if you say so in a word." Lupius responded, "*Ceve*
(move)! I say it. Now, move it!"

"All night long I possessed a lewd young maiden, whose complaisant, demeanor it were impossible to excel. Exhausted with a thousand modes of love, I asked for the puerile service, which she granted at once before I had finished my asking."

The same (XI, 104) reproaches his wife as follows:

"You refuse to pedicate; yet Cornelia allowed it to Gracchus, Julia to Pompey, and Portia did it for Brutus. Ere the Dardanian Cupbearer served the wine, Juno herself acted Ganymede for Jupiter."

Tullia permitted the same to Aloisio and Fabrizio, in Luisa Sigea; we have quoted the passage. Crispa tastes the same variety of pleasure, in *Epigram* LXXI of Ausonius:

"She lets herself be done in either orifice."

The ancient Greeks took great delight in the posterior Venus. One can scarcely express what fervent admirers they were of beautiful buttocks; it went so far, that young girls competed in public, before an assemblage sitting as it were in another "Judgment of Paris" to pronounce which of them was the most gifted in that respect. Athenaeus (XII, 554) informs us that in the environs of Syracuse a villager had two daughters who often quarrelled as to which of them had the finest posteriors; one day they showed them on the highway to a young man from Syracuse, who chanced to be passing, and asked him to adjudicate between them. He decided in favor of the elder sister, fell at once violently in love with her, and on his return home he told his younger brother what had befallen him. The latter went forthwith to see the two girls, and became enamoured of the younger. Soon they got married to the two youths, who were opulent, and they were called by their fellow-citizens the *Calli-pygi,* because, although of lowly birth, their posteriors served them for a dowry. Full of gratitude, they dedicated a temple to Venus, under the title of Venus Callipygos (Venus of the beauteous buttocks).

It will not surprise you, that any young girl remarkable for her beautiful posteriors among her companions was all the more in request for the puerile office, and all the more disposed to lend herself to it. Mania consented to it in favor of Demetrius, as testified by Machon, in Athenaeus (XIII, 579), when the king wants to enjoy her buttocks, she accepts his gift, and says:

"Son of Agamemnon, it is now *your* turn to have them." (25)

A certain young man, Ponticus by name, exacted the same corollary in the morning from Gnathaenion, whom he had possessed all night; it is again Machon who tells us the story (*ibid.,* XIII, 580-81). Demophon, the minion of Sophocles, asked the same favor of Nico (26) who being famed for the beauty of her buttocks,

---

(25) To understand this, the sentence must be complete; the worthy Forberg takes his readers for too learned; Mania, in the poem of Machon, says to Demetrius, offering her buttocks:
"Son of Agamemmon, it is now *your* turn to have them,— you who have ever been so liberal with your own." [*Note of the translator.*]
(26) The following is the passage from Machon, as quoted by Athenaeus; without a knowledge of it Forberg's allusion remains obscure:
" . . . Demophon, Sophocles' minion, when still a youth had possessed Nico, already old and surnamed the she-goat; so-called because she had once devoured that tall

—"she is said to have had an exceedingly beautiful
bottom"—was afraid he might lend them to Sophocles
(*ibid.*, XIII, 582). Gnathaenion (*ibid.*, XIII, 582) made
an ingenious excuse for having been similarly complaisant. A certain coppersmith having ungenerously
boasted he had five times running mounted that little
courtesan in that way, Andronicus, whom she preferred to everybody else, got to hear it, and reproached her bitterly for having allowed such a black-
guard to enjoy her so often, for though he had asked
for that favor, she had never granted him that position. Gnathaenion replied that, not caring to have her
breasts handled by a fellow black with dirt and soot
up to his mouth, it had appeared to her better to take
that posture, so as to touch only that part of his person
which projects farthest and is the smallest. Plate
XXVII of the *Monuments de culte secret des dames
romaines* presents the picture of a man pedicating a
woman.

It is, however, not without some inconvenience, or
even danger, that one lends oneself to the passive part.
Luisa Sigea, Past Mistress in the Sciences of Love,
enlightens us on this point:

"In the first place intolerable sufferings are inflicted
upon the patient, for in most cases he is invaded by
too large a stake; hence frightful infirmities, incurable
by all the art of Aesculapius. The confining muscles

---

lover, Thallos (i. e., Greenbranch—and goats love to eat
green branches) . . . they say she had very fine buttocks.
One day, he begged of her to lend them to him. 'Very
well, she said with a smile—'Take them from me, and
pass them on to Sophocles.' " [*Note of the Translator—
edited.*]

are ruptured, and consequently the excrements cannot be held back, and escape. What could be more disgusting? I have known noble ladies afflicted with cruel maladies to such a degree by eruptions and ulcers, that it took them two or three years to recover their health. I myself (Tullia) have not escaped scot-free from the accursed embraces of Aloisio and Fabrizio. When they first forced their darts in, I endured atrocious pain, but soon the feeling of slight titillation consoled me ... When however I reached home again, I felt a burning pain at the place they had lacerated; I felt myself consumed by an itching as if I were on fire, and in spite of the nursing of Donna Orsini, it cost much trouble to extinguish that confounded fire. If my lacerations had been neglected, I should have died a miserable death." (*Dialogue* VI).

You understand now why the young slave of Naevolus (Martial, III, 71) had pain at the anus; why the same (Martial, VI, 37) says Carinus' posteriors had to be cut; and where the sting lies in the following distich:

"You, who know all the reasons and weighty arguments of the sects,—come tell me, what dogma is it bids you be perforated." (IX, 48).

This effeminate philosopher, who affected to speak as though he had been the successor and heir of Pythagoras, was indeed bound, if anyone was, to know the reasons of lacerations (27) of the anus, and the weights of men's members. He was accustomed to the passive part, of whom Ausonius says in mockery,

---

(27) *Secta*, sect (from *sequor*) may also be derived from *secare*, to cut, and thus mean: laceration. [*Note of the translator.*]

as we saw a little above, that his *clazomenae* served as an anvil:

Men preferred to be supposed *pedicators* rather than *patients;* hence Martial's witty epigram:

"It is now many a long day, Lupus, that Charisianus has been saying he cannot pedicate. But whenever his friends asked him why, he said his bowels were relaxed." (XI, 88)

Would you see the picture of a man engaged in pedication? He is being interrupted in the midst of his business, but the drawing is not the less pleasant for that. The engraving belonging to chapter III of the third part of *Félicia,* presents this position.

Who does not know that the Greeks and Romans were intrepid pedicons and determined cinedes? In the Greek and Latin authors, to the indignation of the pedagogues, the male Venus parades on every page:

"All burnt with the same fire"—we are quoting Luisa Sigea, and we could not express ourselves better or more elegantly. We are, however, going to make annotation to this extract,—"all burnt with the same fire, the common people, the higher classes, the King. This depravity cost Philip, King of Macedon, his life (28); he died by the hand of Pausanias, whom he had

(28) Justinus (t) tells the tale somewhat differently: "Pausanias had had to undergo since his puberty the violence of Attalus, who added to this indignity a crying outrage: having invited him to a feast and made him drunk, he not only satisfied upon him, when full of wine, his brutal lust, but allowed him to be used by all the guests like a vile courtesan, and made him the laughing stock of his equals. Unable to bear this infamy Pausanias carried his complaint before Philip and many and many a time, but the king always put him off with illusory promises. When Pausanias however saw Attalus elevated to the rank of the Chief of the Army, his fury turned against Philip, and the ven-

outraged. It subjected Julius Caesar to the passion of
King Nicomedes (29),—Caesar, 'wife of all men, and
husband of all women.' (30).

---

geance which he could not take upon his enemy, he took
upon the iniquitous judge." (IX, 6).
(t) Justinus (2nd century AD) published an abridgement of
the *Historial Philippicae* of Pompeius Trogus; the original
work is now lost.
(29) Suetonius (*Julius Caesar*, 49): "Not content with having written in some of his letters that Caesar was conducted by the guards to the bed-chamber of the King,
slept there in a golden bed hung with purple, and that he
allowed the virginity of this son of Venus to be lost in
Bithynia, Cicero said to him one day in the midst of the
Senate, where Caesar was defending the case of Nysa, the
daughter of King Nicomedes, and spoke of his obligations
to that King: 'Pray, let us pass over all this; it is only too
well known what he gave you, and what you gave him in
return.'"
On the day of his triumph over the Gauls, among the
bantering songs which are usually sung behind the triumphal car, his soldiers sang the following verses, which
became a by-word:
"Caesar has subdued the Gauls, and Nicomedes, Caesar:
this day is Caesar triumphant for having subdued the
Gauls, and Nicomedes, who subdued Caesar, has no
triumph."
Catullus (*Carmina*, 57, 1-2):
"How well they go together, those shameless cinedes,
Mamurra the patient, and Caesar."
(30) Suetonius (*Julius Caesar*, 51):
"Not yet did he respect the conjugal bed in the provinces;
this appears from the couplet, also sung by the soldiers at
the triumphal entry:
'Citizens mind your wives; here is a bald-headed adulterer.
You indulgently wasted gold in Gaul; this, you take in
return.'"
The same author (*Julius Caesar*, 52) says: "Helvius Cinna,
tribune of the people, admitted to many people, that he
had drawn up and kept ready a law by the instructions of
Caesar, to bring it forward during his absence, by which

"Augustus did not escape this shame (31), Tiberius
(32) and Nero gloried in it. Nero married Tigellinus
(33), and was himself espoused by Sporus (34). Trajan

---

he would be at liberty, with a view to leaving offspring, to
marry whom he would and as many wives as he wished.
So that nobody should be in any doubt about the notoriety
of his lewdness and infamy, Curio, the elder, in one of his
pleadings, calls him the husband of all women, and the
wife of all husbands."
(31) "Sextus Pompeius reproached him for being effeminate, and Mark Anthony says he bought his adoption from
his uncle (or rather his great-uncle) by prostituting himself
to him ... On a day of public games all the people
applauded, taking as directed toward him the following
verse, spoken on the stage of a priest of Cybele, Mother of
the Gods, who was playing a tambourine:
'See you how a cinede governs the world with a finger?"
(Suetonius, *Augustus*, 68).
A picture representing Augustus playing the part of a
patient is in the *Monuments de la vie privée des douze
Césars,* pl. VI, and another of Caesar and Nicomedes, pl.
I.
(32) "It is even said, that during a sacrifice, he could not
restrain himself, smitten with the pretty face of the in-
cense-bearer; the divine service barely finished, he took
the youth aside, and debauched him, and then did as
much for his brother, who played the flute. Soon afterwards he ordered their legs to be broken, because they
reproached each other with their infamy." (Suetonius,
Tiberius, 44). The act of this madman is represented on pl.
XX, in the work of d'Hancarville, cited above.
(33) And also Pythagoras. "One would have thought that
nothing was left for him in the way of debauchery, and
that he had reached the limits of depravity, if he had not a
few days later chosen out of this infamous herd a certain
Pythagoras, whom he took for his husband with all the
solemnity of a marriage. The *flammeum* was put on the
Emperor's head, witnesses, to give away the bride were

(35), the best of rulers, was accompanied by a *paeda-gogium,* while he marched from victory to victory through the Orient. What he named his *paedagogium* was a troop of pretty lads, well developed, whom he

---

present, neither dowry nor nuptial torches were forgotten; all was done openly, even those things, which, if done with a woman, are hidden by the night." (Tacitus, (u) *Annals,* XV, 37). The man called Pythagoras by Tacitus, appears to be the same to whom Suetonius (*Nero,* 29), gives the name of Doryphorus, either on account of his services, or by mistake: "He took for husband the freed-man Doryphorus in the same way in which Sporus had taken him himself for husband, and he counterfeited the cries and sobbings of virgins when losing their maiden-head." Plate XXXVIII of the before-quoted work shows an illustration of this anecdote.

(34) "He went so far as to try to change a young man into a woman; his name was Sporus, and he had him castrated; having given him a dowry, he caused him to be brought to him with the *flammeum* on his head, and married him with all the nuptial solemnities. There has come down to us an appropriate saying on somebody's part, namely, whether it might not have been better for human kind if Domitius, his father, had married a woman of that sort. He made Sporus dress himself in the costume of the Em-presses, and had him carried in his litter; he travelled with him in that way, taking him through the meetings and markets in Greece, and soon after in Rome, around the Sigillarian quarter, kissing him from time to time." (Sue-tonius, *Nero,* 28). Plate XXXIV in the repeatedly quoted French work, gives a representation of the abominable wedding.

(35) "He (Hadrian) enjoyed the affection of Trajan, but this did not save him from the malevolence of the pedagogues of the young boys Trajan loved so ardently." (Spartianus, *Hadrian,* II, 7-8).

(u) Cornelius Tacitus (c54-c117), well known Roman his-torian. Only parts of his *Historia* and *Annales* have survived.

called day and night to come to his arms. Antinous
served as mistress to Hadrian,—a rival to Plotina, but
more fortunate than she was (36). The Emperor
mourned over his death, and placing the dead man
among the Gods, he raised altars and temples in his
honor. Antoninus Heliogabalus, nephew of Severus,
was accustomed, an old author says (37), to have

----

(36) "He lost, during his navigation of the Nile, his dear
Antinous, and wept for him like a woman. There are
sundry allegations about this Antinous; some say he was
devoted to Hadrian, others point to the beauty of his
shape, and to the pleasure Hadrian experienced with him.
At the instance of Hadrian the Greeks placed him in the
ranks of the Gods, and affirmed that he gave oracular
decisions; those oracles, it is said, were composed by
Hadrian himself." (Spartianus, *Hadrian*, XIV, 5-7). St.
Jerome (v) says in the *Hegesippus*: "Antinous, a slave of
the Emperor Hadrian, after whom a circus was named the
Antinoian, founded also a town bearing his name (Antin-
oia), and established an Oracle in the temple."
(37) "Who, indeed, could put up with a ruler who imbibed
pleasure through all the cavities in his body? Not even a
beast of this sort would be tolerated. At Rome his only
care was to send out emissaries, who had to look out for
and to bring to the court men with particularly large
organs for his enjoyment. He had a performance of the
fable of 'Paris' in his palace, played the part of Venus
himself, and suddenly dropping his clothes, he appeared
naked with one hand on his chest and the other covering
his pudenda; he then knelt down and offered his raised
buttocks to his pedicon. He further copied the expression
which is usually depicted on the face of Venus in paintings, and he had his whole body depilated. . . . He loved
Hierocles to such a degree as to kiss his virile parts, a
thing I blush to report; he said that he thus celebrated the
Floralia (a festival held Apr. 28-May 3 when lewd plays
were often performed) (Lampridius, *Heliogabalus*, V, 2-5;
VI, 5)." He did not hesitate to repeat the infamous wedding of Nero with Pythagoras: "Zoticus had such power
over him that the principal officials of the state treated

pleasures administered to him through all the orifices
in his body; his contemporaries looked uoon him as a
monster. Before this Venus, grave philosophers danced
in company with pederasts. Alcibiades and Phaedo
slept with Socrates (38), when they wanted to get their

―――――――

him as though he really were the husband of the Emperor...
He married him, and made him consummate the marriage
in the presence of the giver-away of the bride, telling him,
'Impale me, Magirus!' And this was done at a time when
Zoticus was ill." (Lampridius, X, 2, 5-6). Zoticus, an
athlete from Smyrna, was called Magirus on account of the
profession of his father, who had been a cook.
(v) St. Jerome (340-420) (Hieronymus), best known for his
rendering of The Bible into Latin (the Vulgate). He also
wrote a great many letters which survive and *De Viris Illustribus* (Concerning Illustrous Men)—modeled after a
work by the same name written by Suetonius. *Hegisippus*
is chapter XXII of this work.
(38) Socrates, as is well known, has not been in want of
warm defenders; Brucker (*Critical History of Philosophy*,
I, pp. 539, 540), may stand for all of them. Undoubtedly
Plato (w), in the *Symposium*, brought in Alcibiades, who
says he recollects, to use the expression of Cornelius Nepos
(x) (*Alcibiades*, 2) "to have passed a night with Socrates,
but not otherwise than a son might with his father." But
Xantippe, and it is not surprising, was indignant that her
husband should be on such familiar terms with a good-
looking youth like Alcibiades; and Aelian (y) (*Variae
Historiae*, XI, 12), relates that she stamped upon a cake
sent by Alcibiades, which made Socrates laugh and cry
out: "What are you doing? You cannot eat it now. I do not
care for it at all!" But Socrates! good morals and such
friends are incompatible. Enough to name amongst the
disciples of Socrates, Plato, whom Diogenes Laertius (z)
(III, 30), declares to have loved Aster, Phaedrus, Alexis,
and before all Dion; he quotes an epigram of Plato on
Dion, ending thus:
"O you, who have so fiercely burnt my heart with love,
you Dion!"

tutor into good humor. It is from this kind of amours
practised by the venerable man, that is derived the
erotic phrase: to love *Socratically*. Every action and
every word of Socrates were held as sacred by all sects
of philosophers; they built a temple and erected
an altar in his honor; all his actions had legal
force, and his words the authority of an oracle. The
philosophers did not turn away from the example set
by their Hero (for Socrates took rank with the Heroes)
and new national divinity. Lycurgus, the Spartan le-
gislator, living some centuries before Socrates, refused
the title of a good and deserving citizen to any man
who had not a friend that served him as a concubine.
He willed it that virgins should perform naked on the
stage, so that the view of their charms freely exposed,
should dull in men that sensual longing which by the
aid of nature draws them to women, that they might
thus reserve all their passion for their friends and
companions. For what men see every day loses half its
effect.

_____

(w) Plato (428-348 BC). One of the greatest and best
known philosophers. "Platonic Love" is a by-word today,
and is generally misunderstood to mean love without sex;
in the *Symposium* he advises moderation, not abstinence,
in physical relations.
(x) Cornelius Nepos (94-24 BC), a Roman historian; author
of *De Viris Illustribus*—of which little remains—a sort of
prototype of Plutarch's famous *Parallel Lives*.
(y) Claudius Aelianus (2nd century, AD), called "The
Sophist." A Roman, he wrote in Greek, and left, besides
the *Variae Historiae* (much of which has been lost), *De
Natura Animalium*, a collection of curiosities.
(z) Diogenes Laertius (or, Diogenes of Laerte, a town in
Cilicia) (2nd century, AD). He wrote in Greek of the lives
and ideas of the Greek philosophers.

"Again, why speak of the Poets? (39) Anacreon (40), was hotly in love with Bathyllus; almost all pleasantries of Plautus have this subject for their aim; they are of this kind:

" 'I shall do like the lads, I will cower down over a hamper' (41).

_____

(39 Valerius Maximus (aʼ) (IX, 12, 7) relates of Pindar: "One day, at the Gymnasium, Pindar, leaning his head against the breast of a young lad, whom he loved above all (Suidas says his name was Theoxenes), fell asleep; no sooner had the head of the establishment seen him asleep than he ordered all the doors to be closed, for fear of the poet being awakened." Athenaeus on his part (XIII, 603) tells us of Sophocles: "Sophocles loved boys to the same degree as Euripides loved women;" and a little farther on (604) he relates the story of a youth whom Sophocles enjoyed, but at the price of his mantle, which the rogue abstracted. Euripides, having been informed of this adventure, mocked the poet for having been thus done: "I also," he said, "have had him, but he got nothing else out of me." I am surprised that this passage of Athenaeus should have appeared doubtful to the celebrated Casaubon, on account of the expression "got out of me" which is quite correct and applicable. Sophocles and Euripides had both lavished their white fluids upon the little rogue; but from one of them he got besides a mantle, from the other nothing else.
(40) "No less fiercely burned the love of Anacreon of Teos (bʼ), they say, for the Samian youth Bathyllus." (Horace, *Epodes*, XIV, 9-10).
(aʼ) Valerius Maximus (early 1st century, AD), a Roman historian whose work, *Factorum et Dictorum Memorabilium Libri*, is made up of extracts from earlier historians, many of whose works survive only in these extracts.
(bʼ) Anacreon (c550-c464). A writer of high-quality poems about wine and love.
(41) The actual words of Plautus are:
"I must do the puerile service: I will cower down over a hamper" (*Cistellaria*, IV, sc. i, v. 5),

"Or again:

———

—which means, I will bend down to the hamper, raising
the buttocks, and thus present them to the pedicon. This
is, in fact, what is called, the "puerile office," and which
Apuleius (*Metam.* III, 20), calls "the puerile corollary."
Martial (IX, 68) says simply, *"illud puerile." Conquines-*
cere is according to Nonius (c´) (p. 531, Gottfried's edition),
to curve the spine, an expression designating in particular
the passive posture as we have seen in the *Pseudolus*:
"As soon as he cowers down (curves the spine), then
wriggle your buttocks in time to him."
Some authors have also used a still more forcible expression, *"Ocquinescere,"* viz., "to cower low down" (Nonius,
p. 567). Pomponius (d´), on the word *"Prostibulum"*: "I
have never forced pedication upon any citizen; I have always abstained, unless the patient had asked me and cow-
ered down of his own free will." And on word *"Pistor"*:
"Unless somebody anticipated my desires, willingly crouching down so that I could do the thing securely. "This position of the patient cowering down is very rarely alluded to;
the question generally turns upon his kneeling. "Thus," says
Lampridius of Heliogabalus, "he offered himself with the
buttocks raised to the pedicon." (5). Heliogabalus was
kneeling, and not crouching. The same is the case with
Timarchus in Lucian: "All that were near you remember
it; they have seen you on your knees, while your accomplice did—you know what." (*Apophras*, p. 152, vol. VII.
—Works of Lucian edit. by J. P. Schmid). If you would
like to see these two postures, you will find them in the
Monuments de la vie privée des douze Césars, pl. XXVII.,
a patient crouching, and pl. XXXVIII, a patient kneeling.
From the fact that men wanting to void their excrement
when out of doors cower down, it has come about that
passive pederasts were said to relieve themselves,—in fact
to relieve themselves of the active party's member as it
goes in and out of the anus. Hence in the *Priapeia* (LXIX):
"Look at me, thief, and realise the weight of the member
which you will have to evacuate."
Martial (IX, 70) also plays on the word:
"When you love a woman, Polycharmus, you always re-

'The soldier's poniard did it fit your sheath?' (42).

"That grand master of the art of poetry, Maro (e'), who won the surname of Parthenius by his shyness and innate modesty, cherished a certain Alexander, whom Pollio had given to him as a present, and he has celebrated him under the name of Alexis (43). Ovid suffered from the same malady; he however preferred young girls to lads, because in his amusement he wanted reciprocal pleasure, and not a selfish enjoyment. He said he loved the pleasure 'of the simultaneous ejaculation of both parties' (44), and for this reason he was less given to the love of boys.

"Young girls and wives finding themselves neglected, the first by those they loved, the other ones by their husbands, instead of offering their services only as

---

lieve yourself before you have done. Tell me, Polycharmus, what you do, when you pedicate?"

(42) (*Pseudolus,* IV, sc vii, 85).

(43) You might very well, Luisa, have quoted Horace too (*Epodes,* XI, 23-26):

" ... Now Lyciscus holds me in love-bonds, from which neither friendly advice, nor humiliating afffronts avail to liberate me."

And (*Satires* I, ii, 116-119):

"When your privates are swelling, if some maid-servant or slave-boy is at hand for you to assail forthwith, do you choose rather to burst with desire? Nay! not I!"

(44) (*Art of Love,* II, 683,684).

(c') Nonius Marcellus (early 4th century, AD). Roman author (born in Africa). He wrote *De Compendiosa Doctrina,* a manual of grammar and miscellaneous topics.

(d') Pomponius Porphyrio (early 2nd century, AD), a Roman grammarian who composed a commentary on Horace, little of which survives.

(e') Maro. This is Publius Vergilius Maro (70-19 BC), known as Vergil (or, wrongly: Virgil), author of *Eclogues,* *Georgics* and the well-known *Aeneid.* Asinius Pollio was his first patron.

females, resolved to play the part of the lads. The
depravity became so great that this complaisance was
actually extorted from brides, as it was before from
married women; in fact the husband went at the
young wife pederastically, and the two sexes were
joined in one and the same body. In the facetious
poems of the ancients, Priapus (45) threatens every
thief of vegetables from his garden that comes near
his weapon, that he will take what in the first night
the bride accords to her ardent husband, for fear that
he may wound another part.

"Making use of his imagination with the licence ever
granted both to painters and poets, Valerius Martial
(46) pretends to hear his wife grumble that she also

---

(45) (*Priapeia*, III).
(46) (XI, 43):
"Catching me with a boy, you harass me with your cries,
and you tell me, my wife, that you have posteriors too.
Many and many a time did Juno say the same to Jupiter
the Thunderer; yet he continued to sleep with slender
Ganymede.
He of Tyrius, laying his bow aside, bent Hylas under him;
think you therefore that Megara was without buttocks?
Daphne, by her flight, vexed Phoebus, but his love's ardor
found relief in the end in the boy Oebalius. Although
Briseis slept, often with her back turned upon him, his
smooth-skinned friend Patroclus was more to the taste of
the son of Aeacus (f). Cease then, wife, to call your affairs
by masculine names; better consider you have two vulvas."
His Epigram (XII, 97) treats of the same matter:
"Knowing as you do the honest walk and fidelity of your
husband, and that he never misuses your bed with concubines, why, foolish woman, torment yourself about those
venal boy lovers,—brief and fugitive is the pleasure from
their complaisance!
They are more useful to you than to their master, I tell
you, for they make him think that one wife is better than

had buttocks, and that he had no need of boys. 'Juno,'
she says, 'also pleased Jupiter from that side.' The poet
is not to be convinced, he answers her that the part
taken by a boy is one thing, and that of the wife
another, and that she ought to be satisfied with hers.

"Under the name-boards (47) and the lamps (48) in

---

they all. They give what you will not give;—But I will,
you say, so that the volatile husband stray not from the
conjugal bed.
But it is not the same thing, I want a chia not a mascura
(g'), and you must know theirs is a chia, yours a mascura;
Look! a matron, a woman like you, must know what
belongs to her. Leave to boys what is theirs, and do you
make the best of what is yours."
(47) Some prostitutes sat (Plautus, *Poenulus*, I, ii, v. 54),
others stood: "Another man will only have the harlot that
stands upright in the foul-smelling brothel." (Horace, *Sat.*,
I, ii, v. 30).
(48) Juvenal's Messalina (VI, 123) prostitutes herself
"under the fictitious name-board of Lycisca." Petronius: "I
saw men gliding in stealthily between the name-boards and
the naked prostitutes; I understood, alas, too late, that I
had been introduced into a brothel." (*Satyr.*, ch. 7). Martial (XI, 45):
"When you pass the threshold of a chamber with name-
board over the door, whether it be a boy or a girl that
greeted you with a smile . . ."
That they changed their names when they became prostitutes is apparent from a passage in Plautus (*Poenulus*, V,
iii, 20, 21):
"For today they were to change their names, and will lend
their bodies for infamous traffic."
(f') *Aeacidae* is the word used by Martial. It means "House
of Aeacus" or descendent of Aeacus—loosely: son of Aeacus.
In this case it refers to Achilles.
(g') Chia: a sharp, pungent fig; Mascura; a fig which is
sweet when fresh, but it is very coarse grained. Martial
probably intends a pun here, for mascurae (plural of
mascura) means hemorrhoids.

the brothels sat (49) boys as well as girls, the first
dressed in the feminine stola, the latter in the manly
tunic, and with their hair dressed like boys. Under the
guise of one sex was found the other. Asia (50) was the
original home of this pest, then Africa got infected,
and soon the scourge invaded Greece and the adjoin-

---

(49) Horace (*Sat.*, II, vii, 48-49):
" . . . Every woman that naked beneath the bright lam-
plight endured the thrusts of a swollen member." Juvenal
(VI, 130-131):
"Foul with the reek of the lamp, she bore to the Imperial
couch the stink of the brothel."
(50) Authors vary on this point. Herodotus (h'): "The
Persians pollute young boys; they have learned it from the
Greeks" (I, 135). Plutarch (i') refutes the assertion: "How
can the Persians be indebted to the Greeks for these
impurities, when all historians are agreed upon the fact
that they had eunuchs before they had ever come near to
the Grecian seas?" (Of the Maliciousness of Herodotus, p.
857, vol. II of Frankfort edition of 1620). Athenaeus:
"Pederastia was first introduced in Greece by the Cretans,
as is related by Timaeus; other authors however have
asserted that the man who first imported that sort of love
was Laius, who, having been hospitably received by Pe-
lops, fell in love with Chrysippus, the son of his host,
carried him off in his chariot, and fled to Thebes." (XIII,
602-3). And who has not heard of the incontinence of the
inhabitants of Sodom?
(h') Herodotus of Halicarnassus (c485-c424), called "The
Father of History,' though he was certainly not the first
historian. He wrote *The Persian Wars,* a study of the wars
between the Persians and the Greeks.
(i') Plutarch of Chaeronea in Boeotia (c50-c120 AD), best
known for his *Parallel Lives* which are studies of famous
Greeks and Romans. He also wrote many essays on a
variety of subjects.

ing countries of Europe (51). In Thrace, Orpheus was
the importer and supporter of this unclean pleasure.
The Thracian women, finding themselves held in contempt . . .

"'During the sacred feasts and the nocturnal orgies
of Bacchus, tore the youth to pieces, and bestrewed the
wide plains with his limbs.' (Vergil, *Georg.*, IV,
521-22).

"It is alleged that in those ancient times the Celts
(52) ridiculed those among them who kept aloof from
this practice; such could expect neither civil employment nor honor. Those, that preserved the purity of
their morals were shunned as impure. 'In a town
where everyone is mad, it is not good to be alone sane,
and by reason of its not being good it is not advisa-
ble.'" (*Dialogue* VI)

---

(51) Particularly in Euboea, the chief city of which was
Chalcis, whence the expression, "Chalcidize," meaning,
according to Hesychius, to pedicate, because masculine
loves flourished among the Chalcidians. "Phicidize" is
another expression for the same thing from the name of a
town now unknown; Suidas: "Phicidize, to be a Pederast,"
and similarly "Siphnianize" from Siphnos, an island in the
Aegean; Hesychius (j') says: "Siphnianize, that is to finger
the anus: the inhabitants of Siphnos are, in fact, given to
the practice of pederastia." We have seen above (Ch. II, n.
21) that the meaning of Siphnianize has been perverted.
(52) Athenaeus (XIII, 603): "Of all the barbarians the
Celts, although their women are most beautiful (it is,
therefore, not surprising that an ardent amateur of fine
women, such as Julius Caesar is described to us, should in
the Gallic Provinces have been not over respectful of the
conjugal bed), enjoy boys more; so that some of them
often have two minions to sleep with on their animal skins.
(j') Hesychius of Alexandria (4th century AD, author of a
lexicon.

This ends our brilliant extract from Luisa Sigea.

Even in our own days (53) the taste for the male Venus has not disappeared, witness the Persians, who are very much addicted to this kind of pleasure, as is related by those who have travelled in their country. Amongst others there is Adam Lhuilier, chapter 15, book V, of his *Itinerary*. If we may trust to Luisa Sigea, the Italians and Spaniards did it; also the Dutchmen, with whom towards the middle of the XVIIIth. century, as J. David Michaelides tells us in his *Treatise on the Law of Moses* (in Dutch, para. 258), this habit was so much in vogue, that the punishment of death was hardly of avail against it; also the Parisians, according to the author of the *Gynaeology* (in German, vol. II, p. 427), a fully competent authority, who adds that in almost all the great cities of Europe there are to be found plenty of people who, either being satiated with the ordinary pleasure, or afraid of infectious diseases, prefer the posterior to the anterior Venus,—the English always excepted, who

---

(53) Pardon me, illustrious Marcus Pullarius, for having almost forgotten you. Ausonius (*Epigr.*, LXX):
"Which Marcus? The one they call the 'cat that catches boys,' he who tarnishes all the purity of childhood, who plies with his back-door tool the rearward Venus, the poet Lucilius' *subulo*, his *pullipremo.*"
Ausonius calls him the pullarian cat, because he hunted after young lads (puelli) as the cat gives chase to birds; he calls him, applying to him the same epithets as Lucilius, whose *Satires* he had the opportunity of reading,—more fortunate in this than we,—a *subulo* (from *subula*, an awl), wanting to make it understood that with his member he transfixed, like a cobbler with his awl, the anus of cinedes; and *pullipremo* (*premo*—to press), from his compressing in his work young lads.

abominate this practice. (k') Not to be forever talking
generalities and never giving definite instances, the
cases of Gonzalvo of Cordova (54) and of Vendome
(55), both of them excellent Generals, have been made
notorious enough by historical documents; to these we
could add other still more illustrious examples, taken
from our own time and made known by a heedless
fame; that of a great author, of a great king, (l') the
father of his country, and of a man, who during his
life gained general admiration by the penetration of
his intellect, and the splendor of his language, and
whose knowledge embraced all branches of knowledge, not only the ordinary ones, but the profoundest
and most abstruse (56)— man who might well pro-

(54) "Menacing with his couched lance some youth (he
was a determined pedicon), he would say he intended to
go to Aversa, a famous town." (Luisa Sigea, *Dialogue* VII).
(55) See the *History of the Eighteenth Century,*" by
Christ. Dan. Voss (in German, Part V, p. 364). As to
pedicons of less exalted position, of whom mention is made
by the widow of Philip first Duke of Orleans, in her
amusing letters (pp. 74, 284, 350), which appeared about
thirty years ago, there are: the Cardinal de Bouillon, the
Chevalier de Lorraine, the Comte de Marsan, Francois
Louis, Prince de Conti. These together with the Comte de
Vermandois, a cinede this last, must rest content to appear
in a mere foot-note.
(56) Do not misunderstand what I say. It is not for an
honest man to sharpen his wits at the expense of another's
book.
(k') Why does Forberg except the English? Probably he
had read no 18th-century English literature—to say nothing of Elizabethan. And he seems ignorant of English
history: Edward II and Piers Gaveston, to name but one
example.
(l') "A great king" is undoubtedly Frederick the Great of
Prussia. The others are a matter for conjecture.

pose the riddle of the Sphinx to his eminent confrere
in whom we delight to admire the power of a truly
Ciceronian eloquence, unknown in Germany since the
death of the great Ernesti. These examples, I say, we
could easily allege, were we not apprehensive of raising, quite contrary to our purpose and intention, a
feeling of odium against the pious memory of most
distinguished men.

Do you wish for any more? Pacificus Maximus (m')
offers a goodly number, both of the active and the
passive parties. (*Elegy*, I, to Paul, p. 107, of the Paris
edition):

"The sole cause of my badness was my master,—the
man my father and mother incautiously entrusted me
to. He was the king of pedicons; not one escaped his
lust, so artful and winning was he. Many a thing I
learned, I had better have left unknown; much did I
absorb through my rectum, much through my lips."

Elegy, II, to Ptolemy (p. 110):

"For you, ungrateful boy, I keep my treasures all,
and no one shall enjoy them but yourself; my mentula
is growing: while it used to measure seven digits, now
it measures ten."

Elegy, IV, to Marcus (p. 113):

"You could not, Marcus, find a better, a more convenient place, in which to meet me; not a spy is here
nor woman can tell tales. Let's do it under the willows
in this verdant meadow; the drooping boughs will
hide us with their foliage. The rivulet will lull us to
sleep with its pleasant murmur, and the bird that

(m') Pacifico Massimus of Ascoli (1400-1500), author of
Hecatelegium, from which these selections are taken.

warbles mid the boughs. Hither come, and glide into my lap, thou that art torment at once and remedy of my desires!"

Elegy, XIV (p. 128):

"One day Etruscus brought to me a youth, so fair as is seldom seen at Jupiter's board: 'I give him up to you,' he said, 'lay hold of him, that he may cling to you both day and night. May the gods grant you love him well; he will be wise if you but pedicate him.'

And I: 'I like this liberty conceded to my passion; I shall always be obliged to you. Be sure this child, good as he is, will be better still in future; he will suck my wisdom in through many places.'

"Joyful he goes, joyful I seize hold of my prey; delay, however short, seems long to me. Oh, father proved in virtue! the one blameless man, the one sage in this great town! The master lays hands upon the lad's posteriors, the lad grasps the master's member. Think you, ye unlearned, he will learn in this fashion? Oh, lucky boy, to have me for a teacher! Oh lucky fate, that gave you such a father!"

Elegy, XV (p. 131):

"If the member is dead, the voluptuous wish is still alive; if the old man can no longer pedicate, he still wants to."

Elegy, XX (p. 139):

"My member is so little, this part of me so dwindled, I almost think I never had one, or that it has disappeared; my finger cannot feel, my eye cannot see it,—fate has been but niggardly to me. I could be your attendant, Cybele, without operation, I need no shard of glass, I am a castrated priest already. And still—it is a shame, but must be confessed; there is no worse

lad than I in all the world. As soon as ever I could, I
served the filthy Venus, for the hand of Pederasts had
drawn me to it; a thousand members and big ones,
churned in my inside, and day and night my anus was
in quest. If only my passive action could have profited
my member, when erect it would have touched my
head, when limp my feet; but nothing did it good, it
never grew. And what I did, perhaps only made it
worse. Every boy likes to see his member grow, get
big enough to amply fill his hand."

But enough of pedication; irrumation is our next
business.

OF IRRUMINATION

CHAPTER THREE

OF IRRUMATION (57)

To put the member in erection into another's mouth
is called to *irrumate*, a word, which in its proper sense
means to give the breast; in fact, according to Nonius
(p. 579, Gottfried's edition), the Ancients called the
bosom *ruma*. The verge, introduced into the mouth,
wants to be tickled either by the lips or the tongue,
and sucked; the party who does this service to the
penis is a fellator or sucker, for with the Ancients
fellare meant to suck, also according to Nonius (p.
547). The equivalent to *fellare* in Greek is *thilazo*, just
as *thir*, and *phir* (*fera*) correspond; *thyllis* and *phyllis*
(*follis*); *thermos* and *phermos* (*formus*) and English
warm; thlibo and *phlibo; thlao* and *phlao*.

---

(57) You see we follow the same general order as in the
Priapeia (XIII). "I warn you, boy, I mean to pedicate
you; with you, my girl, I will copulate. The *third* penalty is
kept for the bearded ruffian."

The Lesbians are believed to be the inventors of this particular nastiness. The Scholiast, in verses 1345-6 of the *Wasps* of Aristophanes, cites Theopompus as vouching for the fact.

This is the reason why the Greeks apply the expression *lesbiazien* or *lesbizein* to those who imitated the Lesbian usages, either as *irrumants,* or as *fellators.* Suidas: "*lesbiansai* (Lesbianize)—to defile the mouth; the Lesbians are in fact believed to give themselves to these shameful acts." The same author says under the word, "Siphnianize—to *Lesbianize,* that is to use the mouth abominably" (58). Aristophanes has employed the word in the sense of *sucking* (*Wasps,* 1345-6):

"Look, how cleverly I kept you away, when you wanted to Lesbianize the guests."

And again in the *Frogs* (1303):

"This Muse cannot have used the Lesbian mode?" (59).

---

(58) Eustathius (a) (p. 741) is very ambiguous: "Lesbianize,—to commit a shameful action."

(59) I do not quite know whether the following passage from the *Ecclesiazusae* of Aristophanes (918-20) refers to this or not:

"Now, unhappy girl, you long for pleasure after the Ionian mode. Besides I think you are a Labda (b), as is the way of the Lesbians."

A fellatrix seems to have borne the name of Labda, by reason of the first letter of the word Lesbianize: but the passage stands quite isolated, for in that of Varro, preserved by Nonius, and referring to the annotation of Joseph Scaliger on the *Priapeia* LXXVIII, where we find:

"Depsistis, dicite Labdae."

the reading is doubtful, and the sense not clear. The verse of Ausonius (*Epigr.*, CXXVIII):

"When he puts his tongue in, then it is a Labda."

But Hesychius has employed it for *irrumate*: "Lesbianize, to defile a man's mouth."

Lesbianize and Phoenicianize are generally used conjointly, as though this practice had been equally common among the Phoenicians. Lucian says in his *Apophras* (ch. 26):

"In the name of the Gods tell me what you are thinking of, when it is bruited about publicly that you Lesbianize and Phoenicianize?"

What the difference between the two may be is not known. At any rate Timarchus, who is so bitterly attacked by Lucian, was a *fellator*, as may be readily gathered from the following. Timarchus having arrived at Cyzicus to be present at a wedding feast, was turned out of doors (*ibid.*, ch. 26), the mistress of the house upbraiding him in these words for the impurity of his mouth: "I would not have in my house a man who must have a man himself!" The passage preceding the above is still plainer and more to the point. What does the man reproach Timarchus with, who has surprised him kneeling before a young lad (*ibid.*, chap. 21), and who says farther on, "that he had seen him at work," if this does not apply to a *fellator?* Besides, what is the meaning of that sore throat contracted by him in Egypt (*ibid.*, ch. 27), where according to rumor, he had been nearly suffocated by a sailor, who fell upon him and stopped his mouth?

---

has nothing to do with this question, as we shall show later on.

(a) Eustathius of Constantinople (late 12th century AD), Abp. of Thessalonica and author of commentaries on *The Iliad, The Odyssey*, etc.

(b) Labda is the Greek letter L. In common usage—and in dictionaries—it is lambda, but labda is correct.

Whence that nickname of the Cyclops (*ibid.*, ch. 28), which was given to him, because one day, when he was lying drunk on the ground, a young man, "with an upstanding stake exceedingly well sharpened," threw himself upon him, to force it into his mouth, as Ulysses did with the eye of the Cyclops, "A new Cyclops, with the mouth open at full stretch, you let him burst your cheeks." It is useless to add to this the passages with respect to those who repel his kisses (ch. 23), or as to the use to which he puts his tongue (ch. 25), for it is doubtful whether they are addressed to a *fellator* or a *cunnilingue* (a licker of the vulva). That Timarchus was no stranger to *irrumation*, seems implied (ch. 17) by the apostrophe, "Are you not all that?" the more so as previously Lucian's saying: "If any one sees a cinede do or suffer the shameful act . . ." makes it apparent that the active part was also one of the vices of Timarchus. Lucian could therefore justly say of this Timarchus, that he Lesbianized and Phoenicianized, if he wanted to imply by one of these words, "sucking," and by the other, "irrumating." But it is uncertain which of these words means "to suck," and which "to irrumate." But what does this matter? There is no doubt that Lucian intended to make this distinction. Phoenicianize might even be applied to a *cunnilingue* (60), an expression which we shall dilate

---

(60) I do not know whether the nickname of Rododaphne (rose-laurel), given to Timarchus in Syria (*ibid.*, ch. 27), does not mean *cunnilingue*, as by rose is understood the female parts, while the laurel leaf means the licking tongue. This surname had no doubt for Lucian an obscene sense which he would not disclose: "In Syria they call you Rododaphne, why? I should blush to say it."

upon presently. Needless therefore in this place to
give examples of women who allowed their vulvas to
be licked.

Very remarkable is a passage of Galen (c) in book X,
De vi simplicium, in which he makes a distinction
between Lesbianize and Phoenicianize, demonstrating
that the one is more shameful than the other:

"It is worse for an honest man to be spoken of as an
eater of excrements than as being a defiler or a cinede;
and amongst the defilers we execrate such as Phoenicianize more than those who Lesbianize. The latter I
consider to be doing what is as bad as the habit of
drinking menstrual discharge." (61)

Galen means by this that the man who uses human
excrements as medicine is considered worse than a
fellator or a cinede; that amongst the fellators the
Phoenicianists are more abominable than the Lesbian-
ists. There can therefore be no doubt that he designates the action of the *fellators* by the word Phoeni-

---

(61) Here is the preceding sentence, which will better
elucidate Galen's meaning: "To drink sweat, urine or
menses is an abominable and detestable practice; human
excrements still more so, in spite of what Xenocrates has
written about their beneficial action when applied in lieu
of ointment about the mouth or throat, or when swallowed. He has also spoken of the absorption through the
mouth of ear-wax. I myself could not make up my mind to
eat of them, though it were to cure my sickness right off.
Of all abominable things the most abominable, I think, are
human excrements."
(c) Claudius Galenus of Pergamum (131-201 AD) one of
the most famous physicians of ancient times and considered the final authority during the middle ages. Author of
many medical works and some on philosophy. For a time,
he was private physician to Emperor Commodus.

cianizing, and by Lesbianizing that of the *irrumants*.
In fact, as he judges those the worst who came nearest
to the eaters of excrements, he could not detest less
those who defile their mouths by fellation than those
who defile the mouths of other people by irrumation;
similarly he could not help holding in abhorrence the
cunnilingues and the drinkers of menses, of whom
more later on.

But the Lesbians found imitators. The inhabitants
of Nola, were in bad repute amongst the Ancients in
that respect; in Ausonius (*Epigr.* LXXI), Crispa, a
fellatrix, is said to practise the business "with which
an unprecedented effeminacy inspired the people of
Nola." However, here is this spirited epigram in its
entirety:

"Over and above the intimate joys of legitimate
love, hateful lust has found out other foul modes of
pleasure, of the sort the loneliness of Lemnos taught
the heir of Hercules, of the sort smooth-tongued
Afranius in his actor's gown displayed upon the stage,
of the sort an unprecedented effeminacy inspired the
men of Nola with. Crispa, with but one body, yet
practises them all: masturbates, fellates, lets herself be
done in either orifice,—dreading to die in vain before
she has tried every mode."

To explain,—of course Crispa did not neglect to
have herself entered in the usual way; these are "the
intimate joys of legitimate love." Then she allowed
herself to be pedicated; this is the vice of Philoctetes,
the inheritor of the arrows of Hercules, as also of
Afranius, of whom Quintilian says: "'He excelled in
the Roman comedy; a pity that he polluted his plays
with infamous masculine amours! He thus bore wit-

ness against his own morals." (*Inst. Orat.*, X, 1,100).
Further Crispa did not fail to allow herself to be
irrumated, this is, "the vice their unprecedented
effeminacy instilled into the men of Nola." Lastly the
whole is recapitulated quite plainly in the last line
but one; to masturbate is the genus, while to fellate,
and to work by one and the other orifices are so many
species, three altogether.

There are authors who think that the celebrated
riddle of Coelius in Quintilian: *Clytaemnestram qua-
drantariam, in triclinio coam, in cubiculo nolam* (*Instit. Orat.*, VIII, 6, 53), refers to a woman of the name
of Nola, she being a *fellatrix* after the fashion of the
Nolans. But I prefer the interpretation of Alciatus; he
believes that the woman in question was Clodia, the
notorious sister of Clodius, and wife of Metellus, called
Coa, because she liked coitus on the open triclinium
(d), and *Nola* because she refused the same in bed.
Spalding evinces surprise at the want of exactitude,
which the word *quadrantaria* would have in that case.
To me that appears like looking for knots in a rush.
Why should we not suppose Clodia, disgusted, like
Messalina (e), by the facility of her adulteries, to have

(e) Valeria Messalina, third wife of Emp. Claudius, who
was referred to above (n. 48, Ch. II). In 48 AD she took as
husband Gaius Silius—openly, but without the knowledge
of Claudius, according to Tacitus. Suetonius (*Claudius*,
XXIX) however says that Claudius himself, signed the
contract for the dowry, apparently believing it only a mock
ceremony designed to avert some prophisied catastrophe.
At any event, both Messalina and Silius were executed
shortly thereafter.
(d) Triclinium is both the dining room and the couch upon
which one reclines while eating.

been drawn into extraordinary excesses (62) to such a
point that she would no longer have commerce with
men in the dark, but only in the glare of lighted
torches,—as Martial confesses in speaking of himself
(XI, 105):

"You love the game in the dark ,I like it by lam-
plight; my delight is to make my entry with light to
see by."

—and in the presence of living witness, that she might
be seen, if not actually on her back, at any rate going
away for it or just coming back afterwards. Do you
think that indecency could possibly go farther than
this? What did Augustus do, whom Mark Anthony,
according to Suetonius, "reproached for having at a
festival taken the wife of an ex-Consul from the
triclinium to a bedroom, in the presence of her husband, and afterwards conducted her back to the table
with her face all on fire and her hair in disorder?"
(*Augustus*, 69).

And Caligula, according to the same Suetonius,
"when a guest at a wedding-feast said to Piso, who
was sitting close to him: 'Do not push up so close to
my wife!' and immediately after, made her rise from
table and took her away with him." (*Calig.*, 25) (f).

The same author (*Calig.*, 36), speaking of the most
illustrious Roman ladies, tells us that Caligula "invited
them to dinner with their husbands, passing them in

---

(62) Tacitus (*Annals*, XI, 26).
(f) Livia Orestilla married Gaius Piso; Caligula attended
the wedding and said these words to Piso. Caligula "divorced" her a few days later but would not allow her to
return to Piso, and even two years later, he banished her
on the suspicion that she had gone back to her husband.

review before him, he examined them with the minute attention of a slave-dealer, lifting their heads up if any of them bowed them down with shame. As often as he felt inclined, he left the triclinium and took the chosen fair one aside with him; then after returning to the room with the traces of his doings still upon him, he would praise or criticise these ladies openly, speaking of the beauties or blemishes of their bodies, and even how often he had repeated the enjoyment."

Horace, again, speaks of an adulterous woman (*Odes*, III, vi, 25-32):

"Soon she looks out for fresher adulterous pleasures, while the husband is drunk; and does not care to whom she grants the furtive forbidden pleasures, which with the torches extinguished, she is ready to give and take. Nay! she does not care for her very husband's presence, and with his knowledge she rises to meet whosoever may call, say a merchant, say the commander of a Spanish ship in harbor, who buys her infamous conduct at a high cost!"

Again, look at the feast of the Pope Alexander VI, whom we have already mentioned for your profit and amusement in our *Hermaphroditus* (63).

---

(63) We will here reproduce the curious passage of Jean Burchard (g), to whom we owe this story. It is taken from his *Diarium*, edited by Leibnitz, in 1696 (p. 77):
"On the last Sunday in October the Duke of Valentinois [Cesare Borgia] had invited to supper in his chamber" (the chamber of Alexander VI), "in the Apostolical palace, fifty beautiful prostitutes, called courtesans, who, after supper, danced with the valets and other persons present, first in their clothes, and then naked. After this the table candelabra were placed on the floor here and there with lighted candles, and chestnuts were thrown about, which the courtesans collected moving on their hands and knees

Is this evidence enough to satisfy you as to these *Coae* of the triclinium? Welll it was after this fashion Clodia preferred to be had. Alone with a solitary lover in bed and no one by, she refused (*nolebat*); in public on the triclinium, she was willing enough for coition (*volebat coire*). Hence the jest; she was *Coa* and *Nola*. Coelius might have put it still more plainly; on the triclinium she was *Vola* (willing) in bed, *Nola* (unwilling).

It was not the inhabitants of Nola only who were addicted to the Lesbian vice, the Oscans (64) generally were considered to be very much given that way, so much so that certain authors trace to them (the Osci, in earlier times called the Opsci or Opici), the etymology of the word "Obscene," Festus (p. 553):

"In almost all the old treatises the word is written *Opicum* instead of *Oscum;* it is from the name of this people that shameless and impudent expressions are called obscene, because indulgence in filthy debauchery was very common among the Oscans."

The Ancients employed many forms of circumlocu-

---

quite naked among the candelabra, the Pope, the Duke and his sister Lucrezia being present and looking on. Finally presents were brought in: silk mantles, pairs of shoes, head-dresses, and other objects, to be given to those who had copulated with the greatest number of these courtesans: they were publicly enjoyed in the room there, the lookers-on acting as umpires, and awarding the prizes to the victors."

(64) Nola was a city in the territory of the Campanians. It is for this reason that the *Campanian malady* mentioned by Horace (*Sat.* I, v. 62), has been connected with debauchery, but without sufficient reason.

(g) Jean Burchard (Joannis Burchardi), Bishop of Orta and Civita Castellana. He died in 1506.

tion to convey the meaning of their filthy practices.
For instance, instead of *irrumate*, they said: to offend
the mouth (65), corrupt the mouth (66), to attack the
head (67), to defy to the face (68), insult the head, not
to spare the head (69), to split open the mouth (70),

_____

(65) Varro, in his *Marcipor*, according to Nonius: "He
introduced afterwards into his gullet the virile verge; he
offends the mouth of Volumnus."
(66) Martial (III, 75):
"You make it your work to corrupt pure lips for gold."
And again (II, 28):
"Not even Vetustilla's warm mouth gives you more pleasure."
(67) "How accustomed he was to assault the heads of the
most illustrious women, is plainly evidenced by the death
of Mallonia, who, when brought to him, refused to submit
to his lust. He caused her to be accused by his informers,
and kept asking her during her trial, whether she had
anything to reproach herself with. Without waiting for the
verdict, she ran home and transfixed herself with a poniard, upbraiding loudly the foul, hairy dotard for having
wanted to abuse her mouth." (Suetonius, *Tiberius*, 45).
(68) "He was so glad to have won Transalpine Gaul, that
he could not help announcing some days after, in the
Senate, that he had reached the fulfilment of his wishes, in
spite of the reluctance and groans of his enemies, and that
he would thenceforth be insolent to their faces. Somebody
having said to him offensively that this could not so easily
be done by a woman, he replied jokingly, that Semiramis
had gained a kingdom, and the Amazons had occupied a
great part of Asia." (Suetonius, *Caesar*, 22). Caesar employed the expression: "insolent to the face" in an honest
sense, while his adversary invested it with an obscene
signification, in allusion to his infamous acts in Bithynia.
(69) "I speak of those whose abominable lasciviousness and
execrable lust do not even spare the head." (Lactantius (h),
Instit. Div., VI, 23). Similarly Juvenal (VI, 299-300):
" ... For what cares the drunken Venus? She knows not
the difference between groin and head."

gain the heights (71), mount to loftier regions (72), compress the tongue (73), to indulge in abominable

---

(h) Lactantius Firmianus (fl. c. 325), an early Christian writer and teacher of rhetoric at Nicomedia in Bithynia. Author of *Institutiones Divinae* (Divine Knowledge).

(70) Martial (II, 72):

"They say Posthumus, that they did to you last night, at supper, what I would not have let them do;—who could approve such doings? They split (pedicated) your mouth!"

Then playing upon the words rumor and irrumate he adds:

" ... As the author of this crime, the town's rumor designates Caecilius." And again (III, 73, *ibid.*):

"Rumor denies you are a Cinede."

(III, 80):

"Rumor says, you have an evil tongue."

And (III, 87):

"Rumor says, Chione, that your vulva is intact, that nothing could be purer than it. Yet you bathe without covering the thing that should be covered; if you have any shame, then put your drawers upon your face."

Percidere (to split) employed alone means to pedicate (paedicare). Martial (IV, 48; VII, 62; IX, 48; XI, 28; XII, 35) and *Priapeia* (XII, XIV). Some copies have *praecidere* (to cut off in front) for *percidere*, but this seems to be an untenable reading.

(71) Martial (XI, 46):

"Why do you plague in vain unhappy vulvas and posteriors; gain but the heights, for there any old member revives."

Priapeia LXXIV:

"Through the middle of boys and girls travels the member; when it meets bearded chins then it aspires to the heights."

(72) *Priapeia* (XXVIII):

"A foot-long amulet will pedicate you; if that will not cure you, I go higher."

(73) Plautus, in the *Amphytrion* (I, sc. i, 192):

intercourse (74), and instead of—receiving the
member into the mouth—they said: to lend the mouth
in kind complaisance (75), work with the mouth (76),
lick men's middle parts (77), lick simply (78), or,

_____

"I shall compress today the wicked tongue."
The Latins employed the verb "compress" for *irrumate*, as
if it were a form of fornication; and similarly "split open,"
as if it were a form of pedication.
(74) Plutarch: "It is reported that in the night before the
passing of the Rubicon, Caesar had a frightful dream; he
dreamt that he was indulging in abominable intercourse
with his mother." (*Lives, Julius Caesar*, XXXII). Hesychius' interpretation refers to this: *Arretourgia, aischrour-
gia, kakourgia,*—to perform abominable acts."
(75) Suetonius: "A picture by Parrhasius, representing
Atalanta in the act of complacently lending her mouth to
Meleager, was bequeathed to him with the alternative that
he might have a million sesterces instead, if the subject
offended him. He not only preferred the picture, but had it
solemnly hung in his bedroom." (*Tiberius*, 44).
(76) Horace (*Epode*, VIII, 17-20):
"The member of the uneducated, is it less rigid? Does it
not long, like those of lettered men? To make it stand
superbly from the groin, you need but to work it with your
mouth."
(77) Martial (II, 62):
"A doubtful down did scarcely deck your cheek, when
your tongue already licked men's middle parts." The same
(III 81):
"Baeticus you, a priest of Cybele (*Galle*) what have you to
do with the female pit? That tongue of yours should lick
men's middles (i)."
Ausonius (*Epigr*. CXX):
"When Castor longed in vain to lick men's middles, but
could take no one home with him, he found means not to
lose all pleasure of the sort, fellator as he was; he started
to lick his own wife's organs." In other words from being a
fellator Castor became a *cunnilingue*.
(78) Martial (III, 88):
"They are twin brothers, but they suck different teats: tell
me are they more unlike or like?"

lastly to be silent (79). Just as Persius has employed

The one was a *fellator*, the other a *cunnilingue*.
Again (VII, 55):
"You shall not suck mine, which is honest and small, but a
member escaped from the fire of Solyma (j) and con-
demned to tribute."
I do not know whence Scioppius (k) (*Priap.* X), has it, that
Martial was well-furnished; the latter avows in that passage, that his mentula was quite small. To affront Chrestus, he orders him to lick, not his, but the mentula of a
Jewish slave. He has mentioned this Jewish slave already
in *Epigr.* 35 of the same book:
"My slave carries a heavy Jewish parcel without skin to
cover it." That means, his member is circumcised, the
gland being uncovered, without prepuce, in one word,
"*recutitus.*" So, I think, is to be understood the *recutitorum
inguina Judaeorum* of Martial (VII, 30): he means, "the
virile parts of circumcised Jews," the skin of whose glands
is drawn back. *Recutitus* stands for *recinctus, regelatus,
reseratus.* Many other words, e.g., *revincire,* similarly admit of two meanings, and thus, no doubt should arise
about Martial's expression: *recutita colla mulae* (IX, 58),
which refers to the mules having a new skin covering their
necks. I differ from those who think that those were called
recutiti whose prepuce began to grow again; a *recutitus*
was to the Romans an object of contempt. Petronius: "He
has two faults, else he would be like any other man
recutitus est et sertit,—he is circumcised and snores."
(*Satyr.,* 68). It is impossible to suppose the *glans* could
have been thought more disgusting covered by a new
prepuce than with none at all.
(i) A Gallus can be either a Gaul or a priest of Cybele. The
translator chose "a Gaul," but the priests of Cybele were
always castrated and were noted for their effeminacy.
Martial is saying, "Priests of Cybele are always homosex-
uals. How come you are a cunnilingue, Baeticus?"
(j) Solyma (Solymis) is Greek for Salem, a town in Pales-
tine. But, as this town has no historical importance, the

the word *cevere*, to wriggle, in the sense of flattering,

---

term Solyma probably derives from one assertion as to the origin of the Jews, which is found in Tacitus (*History,* V, 2), that they were the Solymi mentioned by Homer, and that they named Jerusalem (Hierosolyma) after themselves. At any rate, Martial, here and XI, 94, and Juvenal (VI, 543) use Solyma as meaning Jew.

(k) Scioppius (Kasper Schoppe) (1576-1649) published an edition of *Priapeia*.

(79) A man who is being irrumated cannot speak, his mouth being obstructed by the mentula, thus—he is silent. Martial (III, 96) says to Gargilius, a *cunnilingue*, menacing him with the third punishment, if he should catch him in the act:

"If I should catch you at it, Gargilius, I'll make you silent."

Married men were in the habit of pedicating beardless adults, and of irrumating the bearded ones. For which reason Martial warns Gallus (II, 47) to shun the seductions of a famous rakish lady, as he was running the risk, if taken by the husband in *flagrante delicto,* of being irrumated by him:

"Your buttocks you rely on? But the husband is no pederast; he likes but two ways, either mouth or vulva."

And for the same reason he consents to *marry* Thelesina (II, 49):

"No Thelesina for me as my wife! Why?—She is a prostitute. Nay! but she pays young lads. Then I consent."

Then there is a complaint for having been deceived with respect to the lover of Polla, his mistress (X, 40):

"Constantly was I told that my Polla was on intimate terms with an unknown cinede. Well, I surprise them, Lupus: no cinede was he."

Instead of a lad, whom he would have pedicated, he finds a cool, experienced gallant, not at all likely to expiate his crime by means of his buttocks. Martial might, however, have punished him more cruelly by forcing into his fundament, either a mullet (Juvenal, X, 317):

"There are adulterers whom the mullet pierces"; or a radish. "In Armenia, taken in the act of adultery, he ran away plugged with a radish in his posterior." (Lucian, *De Morte Peregrini,*—Works, vol. VII, p. 425). Catullus

so Catullus uses *irrumate*, as meaning to treat ignominiously (80).

It is thus he complains of having been irrumated by Memmius (XXVIII, 9, 10):

"Oh, Memmius, well and long and leisurely, laid on my back all the length of that beam, you irrumated me."

He had, in fact, experienced in Bithynia the meanness and avarice of this Praetor, Memmius, who had not cared a rap for his comrades' honor, and who is alluded to in *Epigr.* X, (12), "Praetor and irrumator." In *Epigr.* XXXVII, (7-8), he threatens his boon companions in debauchery, with whom his mistress has taken refuge:

" . . . Do you think I dare not irrumate alone, as I stand here, two hundred pothouse-heroes?"

――――――――

(XV, 18, 19):
"Drawing your feet asunder, your postern wide open, they will insert into you radish and mullet."
Martial also has used the expression of *being silent*, in the sense as stated, but somewhat more obscurely (IX, 5):
"If in two apertures you can work, Galla, and can do more than double work in both, why, Aeschylus, does she get tenfold pay? She fellates, but that is not a matter of such price, surely. Nay! it is because she must be silent!"
It is not her infamy that Galla sells so dearly; it is the inconvenience of having to be silent during the process, which, for a prattler, "is a very serious matter," as Martial says (IV, 81). Book XII (*Epigr.* 35), quoted later on, also refers to this.
(80) It is the same with the word *stuprum*. Festus (XVII): "The ancients employed the word stuprum for turpitude, as appears in the Song of Neleus—
'*Foede stupreque castigor cotidie.*'
(I am foully and disgracefully beaten every day).
Naevius: "They would rather die than return to their co-citizens *cum stupro*."

And he adds that he would write on the front of the
tavern the infamy of these blackguards:

" ... Your names I shall chalk up all over the
tavern's front."

Other passages of Catullus (XXI, 13, and LXXIV, 5)
are also quoted to prove the various employment of
the word *irrumate*; but they do not seem to me to bear
upon the question.

The epithet *shameless* was especially given to the
man who allowed himself to be pedicated or irrumated. *Priapeia* (LIX):

"If you come to steal, you will return *shameless*."

Cicero (1) (*De Oratore*, II, 257):

"If you are *shameless* before and behind ..."

Horace (*Epistle*, I, xvi, 36):

"If he calls me a thief, he denies that I am chaste."

Lampridius (*Commodus*, X, 1):

"Already as a child he was a glutton and *shameless*", which is explained by what he says in chap. XV
(11): "He gave himself up to the infamous assaults of
young men," and chap. I (7-8): "From his tenderest
age he was depraved, mischievous, cruel, a libertine;
he allowed his mouth to be polluted and defiled."

On the other hand, a woman who had never submitted to a man, was called *chaste* (*Priapeia*, XXXI):

"You are allowed to be as chaste as Vesta."

The same epithet was given to a wife who was
faithful to her husband such a one as is praised by
Martial in *Epigr.* X (63):

(1) Marcus Tullius Cicero (106-43 BC) is generally considered the finest writer of Latin prose. He wrote *De
Oratore*, a book on oratory, many speeches and many
letters. He was executed in 43 BC by Mark Anthony and
Augustus.

"My couch is lighted by the rarest glory,—one member, one mentula alone has known my chastity."

To the preceding examples of *fellators* and *fellatrices* we will now add, from Luisa Sigea's book, that of Crisogono, who cleverly persuades Sempronia to lend him her mouth:

"The day before yesterday" (it is Ottavia speaking), "Crisogono came to see my mother in the afternoon. All was quiet and silent. He had scarcely begun to wanton a little with her, when he became very importunate. 'Yesterday morning,' he said, 'I learned a new kind of pleasure. One of our grand personages, who had certainly tasted it, says that there is nothing so disgusting and repulsive as those parts of his wife which stamp her as a woman,—and he has a very pretty wife, mind! In that sink everything is foul, while in this (kissing my mother on the mouth), dwells the true Venus. He therefore abominates that ill-favored cavern, and adores that pure mouth, that charming head. He looks to nothing else, his member rises for nothing else. His wife is as spirited as she is beautiful, and even more obliging. She knows no other pleasure than her husband's; what he thinks right she thinks proper, and abets all the caprices of her husband; so she lends him the service of her mouth. What would you do, Sempronia, if I asked you? If you were to refuse I should say that you have forgotten all your promises and your pledged faith. You know that Socrates said the beautiful body of a pretty woman is nothing but a living treasure-chamber of voluptuousness, the storehouse whereto men resort to find their pleasures, whereto they direct the burning floods of their lubricity. What matter whether you fulfil your

duty through that pure canal (kissing her mouth), or
through that other (touching below), which is corrupt?' He persuaded her to what she was willing to do
without persuasion. 'Oh!' she said, smiling, 'what an
air you want me to play, and upon what a flute, in our
concert!' taking in her hand his member which began
to rise. She seized the point of his dart between her
lips and turning her tongue around it, caused novel
transports of delight to the member that slid into its
new receptacle. But feeling that the fountains of the
brine of Venus were on the point of bursting forth, she
recoiled with horror. 'You would not degrade me so
far,' said my mother, 'as to make me drink a man in a
liquid form?' She had scarcely spoken, when an abundant shower fell upon her robe. He showed some
anger. 'How could you be so foolish,' he cried, 'as to
spoil such good work!' She replied: 'Forgive me, the
next time you will find me more obedient.' She kept
her word, and actually drank men in a liquid state,—a
spicy thing, for indeed the seed is spicy with salt!"
(*Dialogue* VII).

Mancia also proved complaisant in that way to
Marino; Eleanor tells it in Luisa Sigea:

"My cousin, Mancia, has married a Neapolitan of
the name of Marino. Marino is burning all over with
debauchery. The libertine looks for the woman in
Mancia even above the breasts; he wants her mouth,
as though the vulva of the young wife had taken
refuge there, or as if the mouth had made a bargain
with the vulva to participate in the games of Venus. I
blamed her for allowing so unnatural an act. 'What
would you have?' she said. 'Marino's instrument occu-
pies my mouth, so I cannot complain. We please our

husbands only by reason of being women. Never mind
where she is taken, if a woman only proves that she is
a woman, she will please.'" (*Dialogue* VII).

So too Alfonso tries to engage Eleanor herself in the
same fashion:

"Look you! Ottavia," added Eleanor, "how passionately loving Alfonso is. Some days ago, after having
several times plied his javelin in the legitimate way,
he presented it to my mouth. 'Your catapult, my
Alfonso,' said I, 'is not made for breaching this door;
you are mad, and you want to make me the same.'
'No! I would fain have you mad, not myself; for that
you love me, I owe to your madness, not to any merits
of my own. If I get delirious, I may forget the respect
which I owe you, and I would rather die than cease to
live for you alone.' These words softened my heart,
and decided me to assist him in that game with a good
heart. I seized his inflamed dart between my lips. But
that was all, his member returned voluntarily to the
place it had left, and finished its exploits, which it had
impudently begun above, properly in the region of the
middle." (*Dialogue* VII).

Gonzalvo of Cordova was another amateur of this
mode. Luisa Sigea:

"Gonzalvo of Cordova, a celebrated general, is said
to have taken very much to this kind of voluptuousness in his old age." (*Dialogue* VII).

The prurient ingenuity of Tiberius invented a new
species of *fellation*.

"His turpitude went still farther, to such infamous
excesses, that it is as difficult to relate them as to listen
to them; they are scarcely credible. He caused little

children, of the tenderest age to be taught to play
between his legs, while he was swimming in his bath,
calling them his little fishes, to touch him lightly with
tongue and teeth, and like babies of some little
strength and growth, though not yet weaned, to suck
his privates as they would their mother's breast. His
age and his inclination predisposed him for this sort
of pleasure before all others." (Suetonius, *Tiberius*,
44).

A representation of this ingenious libertine while
tickled by what he called his little fishes, is to be seen
on plate XVIII, of the *Monuments de la vie privée des
douze Césars*.

Men advanced in age, whose member will no longer
obey their will, are more inclined to irrumate than
others. To this circumstance the passage in Martial
(IV, 50) refers:

"No man is too old to irrumate."

(XI, 46):

"Gain the heights; there your old member will revive."

And (III, 75):

"Your mentula, Lupercus, has long ceased to stiffen;
nevertheless, in your folly you strive to make it rise.
You are fain now to corrupt pure lips for gold; but
even so your Venus is stimulated in vain."

For this reason irrumators are less feared by married men. Thus Martial, in the passage (X, 40) quoted
previously, dealt more lightly with Lupus, whom he
had surprised while irrumating his Polla. The husband
of Glycera, if so be that she had one, also need not
have feared that Lupercus would do duty for him

(Martial, XI, 41):

"Lupercus loves the beautiful Glycera; he is her lord and master, and he alone. He was complaining bitterly he had not loved her for a month; Aelianus asked the reason,—he replied Glycera had the toothache."

Lepidinus, in the *Hermaphroditus* (I, 13), is of opinion that anyone who has once irrumated can never get rid of or renounce the habit. I must leave it to experts to decide upon this. So also thinks Luisa Sigea: "Such as have once tasted it, are mad after this pleasure." (*Dialogue* VII).

No wonder that after fellation, the mouth has to be washed out with water. Martial alludes to this (II, 50):

"You lend your mouth, and then drink water, Lesbia; quite right,—where your work is, there you take water."

Priapeia (XXX) says:

"Walk in the vineyards, and if you steal any of the grapes, you shall have water, stranger, to take in another way."

Priapus means: "You came to get water to drink; but if you pluck any grapes, I shall irrumate you, and then you will want water to rinse your mouth rather than to drink." Martial says as much to Chione in *Epigram* III (87), quoted before.

To ask for the loan of the mouth is to demand a thing much more shameful than the other two orifices. Martial (IX, 68):

"All the night long I possessed a lewd young girl; I never knew anyone more naughty. Tired of a thousand postures, I asked for the puerile service; before I had done asking, she turned at once in compliance. Laughing and blushing, I asked something worse than that,—the wanton consented instantly." (81).

---

(81) First the rogue lends her vulva, then her buttocks,
and lastly her mouth. Some suppose the full-bosomed
Spatale of Martial (II, 52) was just as prodigal:
"Dasius was astute at counting the bathers; he asked
full-bosomed Spatale the fee of three women, and she
paid."
But I believe they wrong the good Spatale. Dasius, the
bathing man, wanted only that Spatale, whose charms
were ample and buxom, she taking up as much room as
three other women, should pay for three.
The Phyllis of Martial (XII, 65) showed herself liberal in
every way:
"The beautiful Phyllis, who throughout the whole night
had proved herself right liberal in every way . . ."
From this you will understand what Martial means by
"refusing nothing" (XI, 50):
"I will not deny you anything, Phyllis; for you deny me
nothing."
And similarly (IV, 12):
"You refuse no one, Thais. If you know no shame for this,
blush at least that you refuse nothing, Thais!"
And again (XII, 71):
"There is nothing, Lygdus, that you do not now deny me;
there was a time, when there was nothing you did deny!"
And he says (XII, 80) right out:
"Whoso refuses nothing, Atticilla, sucks."
It is in this sense that Mallonia refused to be entirely at
the mercy of Tiberius; she had already admitted him to
her vulva and anus, but when it came to the mouth the
poor girl could not overcome her disgust. We have before
quoted the passage of Suetonius (m). Of a woman who
refuses nothing, Arnobius (n) (II, 42) says: "That she is
ready to undergo anything," and of a woman that is drunk,
"so much so as not to be able to refuse anything." Ovid
says (*Art of Love*, III, v. 766):
"She is meet to undergo all kinds of assaults."
(m) The Latin indicates that Mallonia refused all over-
tures.

Those who found themselves thus situated took good care not to be surprised; Martial (IX, 45):

"When you have crossed the threshold of a chamber with name on signboard, whether it be boy or girl that smiled on you in welcome, doors and hangings and locks do not content you, and you want to be yet more certain you are not watched. Mystery is what you want; you look suspiciously on the smallest crack in the door and stop it; the same with the tiniest pinhole made by some inquisitive hand. Nobody can be more modest or circumspect in his doings, Cantharus, than the man who wants to pedicate or copulate."

However, the old Romans did not blush to irrumate, as is evident by the use Catullus makes of that word, contemptuous though it be. What they *were* ashamed of was *fellation*. Indeed there is a certain bold audacity in playing the active part, but none in the passive one, particularly when the mouth, the noblest organ of the body, has to perform such vile offices. Add to this that a fetid breath was acquired by this habit, which *fellators* took every means to hide, afraid of putting to flight fellow-guests at table and acquaintances who should greet them with a kiss in the street.

Fellators were so repugnant to the guests at table, that no cups (82) were offered to them, or when they

_____

(n) Arnobius (late 3rd century, AD) of Numidia. At first, violently anti-Christian, he later became converted and wrote a spirited though superficial defense of Christianity in about 295 AD, entitled *Adversus Gentes*.

(82) Martial (II, 15):
"You do not offer your cup to any man; it is discretion, Hermus, forbids, not pride."
And (VI, 44):
"No one, Calliodorus, may drink from your cup."
Seneca: "When Gaius Caesar accepted sums of money for

had been offered, they were afterwards broken (83),
and that it was only with the great unwillingness
anyone would kiss their mouth (84), when presented
for salute. Thus it was preferable to be taken for a
cinede to being taken for a *fellator* (85), like Phoebus
in Martial (III, 73):

"You sleep with youths whose members are full

———

the expense of the games from friends, who brought them
to him, he refused to take a large amount from Fabius
Persicus. His friends not looking at the character of the
sender, but at the value of the sum sent, reproached him
for having refused. 'What!' said he, 'am I to accept the
service of a man from whose cup I should decline to
drink?' " (*De Beneficiis*, II, 21, 5). Fabius Persicus was a
fellator not a *cunnilingue*; this is apparent from the contro-
versy in which Seneca engaged about him as to what a
prisoner should do whom a man promised to buy off, at
the price of having his body prostituted, and his mouth
sullied.
(83) Martial (XII, 74):
"It is no little matter, Flaccus, if you drink with them; and
then have to break the cup they touched."
And Macedonius (o) in the *Analecta* of Brunck (III, 116):
(o) Macedonius (6th century AD), a Byzantine poet.
"There drank a woman with me yesterday, whose fame is
anything but good;—go break the cups, my lads!"
(84) Martial (XI, 95):
"Every time you happen to meet a *fellator's* kisses, I can
fancy, O Flaccus, how you plunge your head in water."
And (I, 95):
"You sang but badly Aegle, when you were loved *per
vulvam*. Now no one kisses you, and you sing well."
And (I, 84):
"Your lap-dog, Manneia, licks your mouth and lips; I am
not a bit surprised; dogs like dirt."
Seneca: "And mark! he made that Fabius Persicus, whose
kisses are shunned even by people who know no shame, a
priest only the other day." (*De Beneficiis*, IV, 30, 2).

size, and what rises with them, will not rise with you.
Pray, Phoebus, tell me, what must I suspect? If I
could think that you were but effeminate! But rumor
says, you are not a *cinede*!"

The case of Callistratus, in XII, 35 of our author, is
a similar one:

"You are very frank, Callistratus, with me, and you
tell me that they often do it to you. You are not quite
so simple as you would appear; the man that tells such
things does not tell of others worse." (86).

For the same reason, as Charidemus will not be
called a *patient*, and shows his legs and chest covered
with hair, Martial tells him (VI, 56) to arrange himself
in such a way as to appear a minion rather than a
fellator:

"Because your legs are covered with bristles, your

<hr>

(85) It appears from Martial's *Epigram* (XI, 98), that the
kiss on the mouth was the regular thing with the Romans;
fellators, therefore, could not be surprised at their kisses
being avoided. The poet of Bilbilis makes yet another
mock at their expense (II, 42):
"Zoilus, why spoil the bath by bathing your bottom in it?
If you would make it still dirtier, plunge your head in."
And (VI, 81):
"You bathe, Charidemus, as though you had a grudge
against mankind, entirely submerging in the bath your
privates. I should not like you to wash your head that way,
Charidemus; and now look! you are washing your head. I
had rather it were your privates!"
(86) In the last verse there are two furtive stings; the first
is about not telling (*tacet*,—is silent), an expression, which
was used as denoting a *fellator*; the second is the word
"tell" (*narrat*), the honorable use of the mouth being put
for the dishonorable, as in *Epigram* (III, 84):
"What tells (*narrat*) your harlot.—No! I don't mean your
girl, Tongilion!—What then?—Your tongue!"

chest with hair, you think, Charidemus, to hand down
your words to posterity; take my advice, and pluck the
hair from all over your body, and get it certified you
depilate your buttocks. Why so? you ask,—You know
the world tells many tales; try to make them believe
you are merely pedicated."

Fellation, as was but fair, received payment, and
high payment. Martial (XI, 66) shows this:

"Informer you are and blackmailer, swindler and
trickster, *fellator* and bully. The wonder is Vacerra,
you have no money."

And again (III, 75):

"Your member, Lupercus, has long ceased to stiffen;
nevertheless, in your folly, you strive to make it rise. Of
no avail is cole-wort or salacious onions, of no use to
you the provocative savory. You are fain now to
corrupt pure lips for gold; but even so your Venus is
stimulated in vain. But,—a thing to be marvelled at
and scarce believed,—what will not rise, Lupercus,
does rise if you pay a heavy fee."

But when on the subject of fellation, we must not
pass over in silence the raven, whom our standing
authority (Martial, XIV, 74), calls a *fellator*:

"Saluting raven (87), why do they call thee *fellator*?

------

(87) You will find in Macrobius (p) (*Saturnalia*, II, 29),
why he was called 'saluting.' Augustus returned as victor
from Actium; amongst those who came to congratulate
him was a man holding a raven, which he had taught to
cry: "I salute thee, Caesar Victor and Emperor!" Caesar,
admiring this flattering bird, bought it for 20,000 sesterces.
(p) Ambrosius Theodosius Macrobius (early 5th century
AD), author of *Convivia Saturnalia*, which, like the *Deipnosophistae* of Athenaeus, is in the form of a dinner
conversation, and which covers a variety of subjects.

Never a mentula entered your beak."

The fact is, ignorant people believed the raven fulfilled the coitus with its beak: Pliny says:

"The vulgar herd believes that it practices coitus and lays eggs through its beak. Aristotle denied this, saying that ravens merely exchange kisses in the same way, familiar to everybody, that pigeons do." (*Natural History*, X, xv, 32-3).

Erasmus (q) denies in his *Adagia*, under the word *Lesbiari* (p. 409 of the Frankfort edition, 1670), that in his time the obscene practice of irrumation was still known:

"*leicharein* (to lick), if I am not mistaken, is with the Greeks the same thing as *fellare* with the Latins. The word indeed remains; but the thing itself has been, I think, long done away with."

I fear this is not really the case. At any rate I am informed that this practice is not entirely opposed to the habits of libertines of the present day; those must decide whose opportunities take them to great cities. Plate XXI, in the *Monuments de la vie Privée des douze Céasars* represents a *fellator*. However the graceful picture in question really belongs more properly to the category of "spintrian postures," of which more anon, than to the present chapter.

(q) Desiderius Erasmus (c. 1466-1536), a Renaissance scholar and humanist.

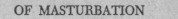
OF MASTURBATION

CHAPTER FOUR

OF MASTURBATION

To excite the member by friction with the hand until the sperm comes spurting out of it is what the Ancients called masturbation, from *masturbare*, that is *manu stuprare*,—to pollute with the hand. This may be done by one's own hand, or by borrowing someone else's. If by one's own, it is generally the left hand that is employed, hence the expression, "left hand whore" in Martial XI, 42):

"You never, Ponticus, enter a woman, but use your left hand whore, making your hand the mistress for your pleasure; think you this is nothing? Believe me, it's a crime, yes! a crime, and worse than you can imagine. Old Horatius copulated once at any rate to beget his three sons; Mars once to get chaste Ilia (a) with twins. Neither of them could have done it, if by masturbation they had procured by the use of their

---

(1) Martial here follows the tradition that Ilia (Aemilia, Rhea, Silvia or Rhea Silvia) was the mother of Romulus and Remus, founders of the city of Rome.

own hand pleasures so shameful. Believe me, that
nature's voice confirms it,—what escapes 'twixt your
fingers, Ponticus, is a human being."

To the same subject also *Epig.* XI, 73 refers:

"Oftentimes, Lygde, you swear you will grant my
prayer, even appointing the place, even appointing the
hour. Longtime I lay consumed with desire, till often
my left hand comes to my help in your stead."

And this passage of book VI of Ramusius, p. 62 of
the Paris edition:

"What are you to do? Is your left hand safe and
sound? Well use it, then you will not want a whore.
Why pay for what your left hand gives you gratis?"

There were of course also people who used their
right hand; the same Ramusius of Rimini (book IV, p.
61) tells us:

"I suffer, dear Donatus, from so frightful an erection, I am fearful for my member, if you do not help
me. My right hand, being wounded, can do nothing; I
have no money; Hylas is not here; no vulva opens for
me—no chance of fornication; appease my desire, that
I may live, and you can do it cheaply."

Pacificus Maxmus (*Elegy* XII, p. 126) Paris edition:

"What shall I do? I am so stiff—I'm bursting, and I
could easily fill three or four large bottles. It is long
since my member has known a vulva, long since it has
stirred the entrails of a man. It is stiff day and night,
and will never relax,—night and day it lifts its head.
No youth, no girl will listen to my prayer, no help—
my right hand must then do the service!"

We have seen just previously, with what severity
Martial reproached Ponticus, a masturbator, for losing
between his fingers the substance of a man. Neverthe-

less this fine moralist did not hesitate to put his own
hand to similar use under the pressure of erection
(*Epigr.*, 43, book II):

"Another Ganymede, my hand assisted me."
and (XI, 73):

"Often my left hand comes to my help in your
stead."

Nor was his severity given to whining when he
exhorted (XI, 58) the cinede Telesphorus:

"Soon as ever you see I want it, and know that I am
in erection, Telesphorus, then you demand a heavy
price,—can I say nay? (88) If I will not swear to pay
you, you will withdraw those posteriors of yours,
which are so precious to me. If with his razor set to
my throat, my barber, while shaving me, demands my
liberty and fortune, I promise all; 'tis not the barber
asks, but a cut-throat, and fear compels me to say
'Yes.' But once I see the razor returned to its curved
case and harmless, why! I will break every limb of the
fellow. Not that I will harm you, but my left hand
once washed, my member will say 'Go hang!' to your
grasping avarice" (89).

---

(88) Martial had made use of the same interrogative
phrase with the verb in the infinitive and *puta* put instead
of *scilicet* also in Epigram III, 26—*Hoc me puta velle
negare?* (Can I say nay to this?). Scholars have found
occasion for a pile of annotations on the two passages:
these need not detain us.
(89) Martial's meaning is: My left hand will console my
suffering mentula; the business done, my hand covered
with the ejaculation of the sperm, like the fleece on the
pubis of Ravola in Juvenal (IX, 4)—if indeed it is the
fleece of his pubis that is intended:
"When Ravola with wet beard rubs the groin of Rhodope"
The greedy cinede will be told to go to the deuce, to

The same when his wife surprised him engaged
with a youth (XI, 43)—a witty epigram quoted previously (note 46, Ch. III), as also when he intended to
marry Thelesian (II, 49) (See note 79, Ch. III):

"Thelesina pays young lads; then I consent."

The same when he recommends somebody, I do not
know who (XI, 22), to make use of the posteriors of
Galesius only, as the part that would suit him:

"Youths are divided by nature; one part is reserved
for girls, and the other for men—use your own por-
tion."

Is what the pedicon loses in the anus of the cinede
anything else but the substance of a man, which the
masturbator wastes between his fingers?

As it is in the nature of the virile member to rise at
the mere sight of a pretty woman's naked body, the
amorous desire in that state often craves imperiously
for relief, for "man in erection is not overwise (b)"
(90). This is why, when the fair one's heavy coverlets
have been thrown back:

"Meantime the adulterer she has sent for lurks in
furtive concealment, and impatient of the delay, yet

---

slink off with drooping head, like the man in Horace
(*Satires*, II, v, 69), who finds:
"Nothing is left to him and his but to weep."
This moist hand reminds us of the adulterous woman in
Juvenal (XI, 186), who
"Shows humid traces in the doubtful pleats of her tunic."
(90) Suidas under the word *estukos*, after Aelius Dionysius
(c) apparently.
(b) A modern variation is: "A stiff member has no cons-
cience."
(c) Aelius Dionysius of Halicarnassus, a writer of the 2nd
century, BC.

says never a word, but pulls his foreskin" (91). (Juven-

---

(91) It was not out of voluptuousness, but for decency's sake
that Jews who had renounced their nation had their
prepuce redressed over the glans, as they did not wish it
to be seen that they had been circumcised, so they took
means to get their bare glans recovered. "And they made
for themselves new prepuces" (*Maccabees*, I. i, 15). "Is
there anyone who has been brought to believe, circumcised? Let him not recover his gland" (*Corinthians*, I, vii,
18). Celsus, *De Medicina* (VII, ch. 25): "If the glans is
bare, and it is desired for convenience sake to cover it, this
can be effected, but more easily with a child, than with a
grown man, more easily with the man born so, than with
the man who has been circumcised after the custom of
certain people." After having explained the method of cure
applicable to men with whom it is a natural accident,
Celsus continues: "With people who have been circumcised, the skin must be detached behind the crown of the
glans. This operation is not very painful as the prepuce
being loosened, you can draw it with the hand back to the
pubis without any bleeding. Then the loosened integu-
ment is drawn once more over and beyond the glans.
This done the verge is dipped frequently into cold water,
and then covered with a plaster, which has a strong
tendency to minimise inflammation ... As soon as it is
quite free from inflammation, the verge is to be bandaged
from the pubis to the corona; the skin is then drawn over
the glans, but kept separate from it by a plaster. In this
way the lower part of the skin grows on again, while the
upper part heals without adhering."
From this passage it would appear that at the time of
Celsus the method of laying bare the glans which afterwards prevailed with the Jews was not discovered yet, by
which, according to Buxtorf (*Dictionnaire Talmudique*),
after the prepuce has been cut away, the circumcisor takes
hold of the remaining skin between the thin edges of his
thumb nails, and draws it forcibly back. If this practice
had been customary it would have been superfluous to
separate the prepuce with the scalpel. I conjecture from

al, VI, 237-8).
and why:

"The Phrygian slaves would be masturbating behind the doors, every time Andromache mounted her
Hector horse fashion." (Martiae, XI, 104).

This is why during the dances of the young Gaditanian (d) girls, which were without doubt very like
the dances that are still so much appreciated by the
Spaniards (92), the limp appendages of even grey-
headed spectators began to move visibly, as many
authors tell us. Martial (VI, 71):

"Cunning in the wanton gestures that go with the
Baetican (e) castanets, skilled in dancing to the Gaditanian measures, she might well stiffen trembling Pe-
lias, and excite Hecuba's husband to emulate vigorous
Hector."

Juvenal (XI, 162-164):

"Perhaps you may wait while the Gaditanian dancer
begins to feel the wanton stimulus of the loud strains
of her accompanying band, and the girls, fired by the
applause sink to the ground with quivering buttocks,

---

this, that the Jews were called *recutiti*, from having this
skin of the glans drawn back, which, not being done, the
circumcision was not considered complete; but Celsus
makes me doubt this.

(92) Julius Caesar Scaliger (f), *Poetica*, (book I, p. 64):
"One of these infamous dances was the *riknoma, rik-
nousthai*, meaning, wriggling the haunches and thighs, the
crissare of the Romans. In Spain this abominable practice
is still performed in public."

(d) Gaditanion, from Gades, modern Cadiz.

(e) Baetica was the province of Southern Spain, where
Gades was.

—a sight to sting languid senses to love . . ." (93).

But it is not only by the sight of a beautiful naked female the member is excited; who does not know that it is also roused merely by images called up by the imagination, particularly in the night. And the power of such fancies is such as to provoke a pleasurable ejaculation of sperm. Priapus himself has experienced

---

(93) Do not miss, reader, the motive of this dance; with their buttocks wriggling the girls finally sank to the ground, reclining on their backs, ready for the amorous contest. Different from this was the Lacedaemonian dance *bibasis*, when the girls in their leaps touched their buttocks with their heels. Aristophanes in the *Lysistrata* (82): "Naked I dance, and beat my buttocks with my heels."
Pollux (g) (IV, ch. 24): "As to the *bibasis*, this was a Laconian dance. There were prizes competed for, not only amongst the young men, but also amongst the young girls; the essence of these dances was to jump and touch the buttocks with the heels. The jumps were counted and credited to the dancers. They rose to a thousand in the *bibasis*."
Yet more difficult was that kind of dance which was called *eklaktisma*, in which the feet had to touch the shoulders. Pollux (*ibid*): "The *eklaktismata* were dances for women: they had to throw their feet higher than their shoulders."
This kind of dance is not unknown in more modern times. J. C. Scaliger, *Poetica* book I, p. 651: "To this day the Spaniards touch the occiput and other parts of the body with their feet."
(f) Julius Caesar Scaliger (1484-1558) Italian physician and Latin scholar who settled in France. Author of Latin poetry, *Poetica,* and father of Joseph Justus Scalinger (see note i, Author's Preamble).
(g) Julius Pollux (2nd century AD), born in Naucratis, Egypt, he was tutor to Emp. Commodus and author of a dictionary.

this. *Priapeia* (XLVIII):

"You see this organ after which I am called by my name Priapus, is wet; this moisture is not dew, nor yet hoar-frost. It is the outcome given of its own sweet will, on recalling memories of a complaisant maid."

It is said that Diogenes the Cynic was a masturbator; once caught in the act of handling his mentula, he said: "I wish to heaven I could in the same way satisfy my stomach with friction when it barks for food" (94).

When the masturbation is done by the loan of another person's hand, it is possible that the pleasure is participated in on the part of the agent.

It forms part of the business of a courtesan to be clever with her fingers; a languid member may by their use be invigorated. The inertness of the virile member may be caused by the inconveniences of age, either on the part of the woman, as in Martial (VI, 23)

"You require my penis, Lesbia, to be ever in erection for you; believe me a man's member is not like a finger. True, you strive to excite me with hands and tender words, but your face is a stubborn fact and counteracts all your efforts."

and again in the same author (XI, 29):

"When you set your old hand the task of rousing my member, your thumb, my Phyllis, will but strangle me."

_____

(94) Diogenes Laertius (VI, 2, 46): "One day, whilst masturbating himself in the middle of the market he said: 'I wish to heaven that I could prevent my stomach from being hungry by rubbing it.'" Plutarch, *De Stoicorum repugnantiis* (p. 1044, vol. II, of his works): "Chrysippus praised Diogenes for masturbating himself in public, and for saying to the bystanders: 'Would to heaven by rubbing

or of the man, Martial (XI, 46):

"Only in dreams you get stiff, (95) Maevius, and
your verge begins to make water right on to your own
feet; in vain your wearied fingers ply your wrinkled
member,—rouse it as you may, it will not raise its
drooping head." (96).

Aristophanes in the *Wasps* (737-40-):

"Yes, I will nurse him and get him all that is wanted
for an old man: beef broth to lap, soft wool, and a rug
to keep him warm, and a courtesan to rub his member
and his loins ..."

The same author (*ibid.*, 1343-44-):

" ... The cable is rotted away, yet is it still fond of
being rubbed."

Nor is it unwelcome to men in the vigor of life, and
who are fit to caress young girls, to have mistresses
whose hands are not lazy in bed, and whose fingers
know how to act in the dark regions where the arrow
of love is hidden. Martial (XI, 104) complains about

---

my stomach in the same fashion, I could satisfy my
hunger.' "
(95) Mark with what minuteness the Ancients scrutinized
nature; with what ingenuity they gave expression to all
their sentiments! Who dares nowadays write such a verse
describing as a natural thing what might be but a solecism
of his mentula.
(96) Bassus, who was in the habit of taking his pleasures
with young minions, long-haired and slim, set the hands of
his wife to work to excite his mentula, when he came back
to the conjugal couch fatigued and languid. Martial (XII,
98):
"You tire yourself, oh Bassus, but with minions, paying
them from the dowry of your wife; thus when you return
to her side, that member bought at the price of many
million sesterces, lies languid. In vain her tender thumb
tries to excite it, vain are her tender words, it will not
stand."

the unseemly gravity of his wife, which forbade her to
render him that service:

"You will not help me on by movement or by word,
nor yet with your fingers, as though you were prepar-
ing the incense and the wine for sacrifice" (97).

Penelope, on the other hand, contented Ulysses well
that way, as Martial has it in the same epigram:

"Chaste though she was, when the Prince of Ithaca
lay snoring, Penelope liked to have her hand always
on it."

Ovid's mistress did him the same service, but all in
vain one miserable night, when a hostile divinity
seemed to have smitten to death that most pitiful part
of him, to use his own expression, and the girl, in
order that the servants might not think that she had
remained untouched, pretended to make her ablutions
all the same (*Amores*, III, vii, 73-4):

"My darling did not disdain even to put her hand to
it and gently try to rouse it."

This virtue of the fingers in procuring erection is
alluded to by Juvenal (VI, 195-96):

"When a seductive voice is worthless and will not
excite your member—the fingers do it."

The author of the *Priapeia* was also well aware of
the fact (LXXX):

"My member is not very long nor very thick,—
handle it, and you'll see it grow apace."

And so was Janus Dousa (h), quoted by Scioppius a-
propos of this same *Priapeia*, cleverly scenting out the

---

(97) The women of Aristophanes (*Lysistrata*, 227) threa-
tened their husbands with a similar rigidity of body:
"Though he may have his way, I shall be crabbed and
never move."
(h) Janus Dousa (1545-1609), a Dutch scholar who wrote
commentaries and edited an edition of Petronius.

man's character:

"Dousa, commenting upon Petronius, informs us
that he knows *by home experience* how this object
grows in thickness and length when massaged by a
woman."

You can estimate the importance of this function by
the value set by the Ancients, as in our days by the
Turks, upon masseurs and masseuses, who are employed for manipulating the joints with artistic expert-
ness, their fingers softly pressing and turning them,
and their hands kept soft by the constant use of
gloves, kneading tenderly all the limbs. Seneca, (*Letter* LXVI, 53):

"Would I rather offer my limbs for massaging to my
superannuated minions? or to some little woman, or
some weakling man, more woman than man, to draw
and crack my fingers? Should I not rather envy yonder
Mucius, who put his hand in the fire with the same
equanimity as though he tendered it to a masseur."

Martial (III, 82):

"A woman massages your body all over with nimble
skill; her trained hand manipulates *all* your members"
(98).

John of Salisbury (i) states in his *Policraticus* (book

(98) He had a hand of no less experience (Juvenal, VI,
422-23), that cunning masseur who put his fingers to the
lady's clitoris.
"And made his mistress's thigh resound beneath his hand
high up."
(i) John of Salisbury (d. 1180), medieval humanist, classical
scholar and author of various philosophical and other
works. A pupil of Peter Abelard, he was for a time envoy
for Henry II of England, but he went to France after the
murder of Thomas á Beckett, and was later Bishop of
Chartres.

III, ch. 13) after some ancient author, perhaps Clearchus (j), as Lipsius (k) thinks:

"When a rich libertine turns in his luxurious ways to effeminacy, a youth with frizzly hair takes before all the world his feet while he is lying on his couch, and massages them and his legs, not to go further, with his delicate hands. That youth is always wearing gloves, so as to preserve them white and soft for the benefit of rich people. Then, using his hands more licentiously, he runs them over all the body with impudent touchings and ticklings, raising the desires and stirring the amatory flames of his employer."

I may very well describe here, for I could not find a better place, a performance for which the friendly hand of a woman is in request, but of a woman who is an expert, which will gently press your testicles and stroke your thighs; it is said that nothing can be pleasanter or more voluptuous. Luisa Sigea describes, with her inexhaustible ingenuity, such a scene, executed by Ottavia and Roberto, with the assistance of Manilia; the fullness, variety and richness of the description, placed in the mouth of Ottavia, are admirable:

"Manilia then conducted us to the trysting place; she undressed me, and placed me naked on the couch. Roberto jumped on to the couch. 'Now,' he said, 'I shall enjoy the most supreme unalloyed bliss. Carried on your chariot, Olympia, I shall take my way through his dark thoroughfare,' (he was pinching my pubis the

---

(j) Clearchus (late 4th century BC), a Greek poet of the Middle Comedy genre.
(k) Justus Lipsius (1547-1606), a Latin scholar at Louvain.

while) 'I shall take my way to glory.' His hands were
straying over my belly, my thighs, examining every
thing. His member was swelling. 'Permit me, my
Venus!' he said, giving me a kiss. 'Willingly,' I answered, 'you shall have me in any way you like.'
Manilia interposed, 'Why so much talk! Do not talk
but act! I will assist both of you, and add new delights
to your voluptuous sensations. You are in excellent
trim, Roberto! Come, down with you upon Ottavia's
snowy bosom, and have your fill!' Roberto precipitates
himself upon me, and his engine strikes against my
belly. Manilia's soft hand intercepts the erring tool.
'Come,' she says, 'you vagrant, enter the lovely prison,
and do the task set to you by your mistress.' With her
other hand she pushes the young man's back, and I
take him in, entirely in. Manilia tells me not to move.
'Raise your left thigh, Ottavia,' she says, 'and stretch
out the other one.' I obey. 'You, Roberto, you now
push gently and quickly! As to you, Ottavia, kiss him
but without moving!' We do so. She added. 'When
you both feel the boiling foam running over, you,
Ottavia, give a sigh, and you, Roberto, gently bite
Ottavia's lips!' He then begins to poke vigorously, but
without haste or violence, in and out; I press him on
to me, kissing him but not moving. I feel it coming. I
sigh. 'Now! now, Roberto!' cries Manilia, 'help Ottavia! Work away!' He shakes me and pounds me. Soon
I feel a slight bite on my neck. I heave a sigh. 'And
now, Ottavia,' cries Manilia, 'you assist Roberto; move
your buttocks briskly, raise up your loins, quick! quick!
Well done, my child! Lais, herself I think, could not
have shown more flexibility or agility!' The sweet
youth begins to ejaculate, and I feel my inside inundated by the fiery spring of love. I moved with body

and soul. I never arrived more quickly at the acme of voluptuousness. Manila caressed with one hand my buttocks, and with the other hand Roberto's; at the same time she pressed with the points of her fingers the lips of my vulva and his testicles, which were close up. The youth swooned, and our nurse withdrew, and clapped her hands applauding!" (*Dialogue* VII).

Plates IV and XII, in the *Monuments de la vie privée des douze Césars*, show you Cleopatra titillating with a delicate hand the virile parts of Julius Caesar and Mark Anthony, while in the *Monuments du culte secret des dames romaines;* plate XVI, represents Livia bestowing the same caresses on Augustus; plate V, a Bacchante doing it to a Faun; plate IV, a masturbator—expressly so called. In plate XLIV of the *Monuments de la vie privée des douze Césars*, again is a picture of a girl helping Tiberius, with her benevolent hand, in pedicating Otho.

Again it sometimes happened that lewd men found pleasure in handling the genital parts of other men. Martial knew nothing more infamous (XI, 22):

"That your coarse lips should receive the delicate kisses of fair-skinned Galesus, that you should sleep with your naked Ganymede—is not this enough yet? It ought to be! Cease at any rate to touch the privates with provocative hand. With boys of tender age this does more harm than the member does. The fingers hasten virility and make them prematurely men. Hence the goaty smell, the quick-coming hairs, and the beard that make the mother wonder, while they no more love to bathe in the open light of day. Nature has divided boys; one side is reserved for girls, the other for men. Keep to the side which is yours."

Martial means to say that the member was given to boys for the purpose of using it with girls, while their buttocks were for the service of men, and that this pedicon should therefore make use of Galesus' buttocks rather than play with his mentula. Of similar import is also *Epigram* (XI, 70) directed against Tucca, who wanted to sell young lads:

"Oh, for shame! there is the groin with the tunic all open, and a member appears fashioned and trained by your hand."

He says it is a crime to put up for sale those lads whom the infamous Tucca has trained for debauchery and to let the buyers see their fully formed mentulas, accustomed to rise under the provocative hand of the master. Eumolpus subjects in the same way the verge of Encolpius to friction. Petronius (chap. 140):

"After these words" (Encolpius speaking) "I lifted up my tunic, and exhibited myself in full vigor to Eumolpus. He first recoiled as if horror-struck; but, like a man who expected worse, he got hold with his two hands of God's gift, viz.: the verge in erection."

I have still to treat, in order to complete my task, of other pleasures belonging to this category, meaning those which can be taken in any interstice of the body. A few words will suffice. Taking in the first place the breasts, I have recourse to Luisa Sigea:

"By the twin conch-shells of Venus!" (*Dialogue* VII, Ottavia speaking) "I am ashamed. I blush to think, that the valley between my breasts has done duty as the avenue of Venus. You know there is in our house a gallery giving on the garden-parterres, which are full of all sorts of flowers. There Caviceo and I were

promenading; he embraced me, kissed me, bit my
lips ... He put his left hand in my bosom. 'I am after
trying a naughty trick,' he said. 'Undress, my darling!'
What was I to do? I undressed. His eyes rested on my
bare bosom. 'I see,' he said, 'Venus sleeping between
your breasts. May I waken her?' While he was talking
he had thrown me on my back in the bed, and being
in a noble state of erection, slides his hot, burning
member between my breasts. How could I escape his
blind passion? I had no choice but to bear it. His
hands softly pressed my breasts together, so as to
narrow the space in which his mentula had to travel
towards a new experience. Why make a long story?
Stupified as I was at this vain ridiculous imitation of
Love, he inundated me with a burning libation: he
had his will."

As to other interstices of the body, e. g., the armpits,
between the thighs, the calves, the buttocks (mind, I
do not say the anus, but between the buttocks), be it
enough to mention Heliogabalus; Lampridius (V, 2-3):

"Who, indeed, could put up with a Prince who
imbibed pleasure through all the cavities in his body.
Not even a beast of this sort would be tolerated."

Also Commodus, according to the same Lampridius
(V, 11):

"He gave himself up to the infamous assaults of
young men, polluting every part of his body, even his
mouth, and that with either sex"—i.e., he was both a
fellator and a *cunnilingue*.

Is it necessary to speak here of the debauchery of
those who assault the corpses of females, or statues?
This is not real coitus, there being no two parties to
the act. Nevertheless, according to Herodotus (II, 89),

in Egypt a man was taken in the act of abusing the
corpse of a woman just dead:

"It is said that a man was surprised in the act of
working in the fresh corpse of a woman, and de-
ounced by a fellow-workman."

In consequence of this a law was promulgated
forbidding the corpses of noble and beautiful women
to be given into the hands of the embalmer until three
or four days after their decease. And who does not
know the story of the Venus of Cnidos, the work of
Praxiteles, as related by Pliny, *Historia Naturalis*
(XXXVI, iv, 21):

"It is related how a certain youth fell in love with
her, and having hidden himself one night in the
temple, cohabited with the statue, leaving a stain as
the mark of the gratification of his passion upon the
marble."

There is a similarity in this with the mistake made
by a bull which, according to Valerius Maximus (VIII,
ch, II) fell in love with a bronze cow, and copulated
with the same at Syracuse, being deceived by the
perfection of the resemblance.

OF CUNNILINGUES

CHAPTER FIVE

OF CUNNILINGUES

We have now said enough about the work of Venus performed by the virile member; it remains for us to explain how a sacrifice may be offered to Venus without one. This may be done by means of the tongue or of the clitoris. We have accordingly first to treat of the cunnilingues, those who lick women's privates, and then of the tribads.

As it is the office of the *fellator* or *fellatrix* to suck the virile parts, so is it the business of cunnilingues to lick the female. The cunnilingue operates by introducing his tongue into the vulva. Martial (XI, 61) has described this monstrous act very clearly:

"Manneius, husband with his tongue, adulterer with his mouth, more foul than the mouths of harlots of the Summoenium; whom seeing, as he stood naked, from a window, the filthy procuress closed her brothel; whose middle she had rather kiss than his head. He who of old knew all the channels of the inwards, and could declare with a sure and certain voice, whether 'twas a boy or girl in the mother's belly (be glad, all vulvas, for your part is done), can no longer erect his fornicating tongue. For lo! as he lurks with tongue plunged in a swelling vulva and hears the babes wailing inside their mother, a shocking malady paralyses his greedy mouth,—and now he can no more be either clean or unclean."

By the same paralysis of the tongue Zoilus was struck; Martial (XI, 85):

"An evil star, Zoilus, has struck your tongue of a sudden, even while licking a vulva. Of a surety, Zoilus, you must now use your member."

Baeticus, the castrated priest of Cybele, against whom Martial has directed *Epigram* III (81), was a cunnilingue:

"What have you, Baeticus, a priest of Cybele, to do with the female pit? That tongue of yours by right should lick men's middles. For what was your member amputated with a Samian potsherd, if the woman's parts had so much charm for you? You must have your *head* castrated; true, you are a castrated Gallus (a) in your secret parts, but none the less you violate the rites of Cybele; you are a man so far as concerns your *mouth*."

If this passage were in the least doubtful, *Epigram* 77 of the same book might offer difficulties, not otherwise:

"Some latent sickness of your stomach I suspect. Why, I wonder, Baeticus, are you an *eater of filth?*"

In fact the *fellator* as well as the *cunnilingue* may be called eaters of filth, as in the passage of Galen quoted previously, where both of them are called *coprophagi* (dung-eaters). Baeticus however has only

---

(a) Gallus (See note h, ch. III)

to do with the female pit; he is a *cunnilingue*, not a *fellator*. On the contrary, the lewd tongue of Tongilion (III, 84) is that of a *fellator*, not of a *cunnilingue*; for the tongue of a *cunnilingue* plays the part of a lover, being active; while that of a *fellator* acts the part of a prostitute, remaining passive. Sometimes for want of attention the most learned commentators are at fault in elucidating these playful passages. One of the twin brothers, who in our friend of Bilbilis (the poet Martial) (III, 88), are licking different groins; was a *cunnilingue*. The neighbor of Priapus, "by whose fault it is unhappy Landice swears she can hardly walk, she is so enlarged," is covertly designated as a *cunnilingue;* (*Priapeia* LXXVIII) yet for all that Scioppius maintains he was only a fornicator; but why should we turn away from the proper sense of the word on account of the enlarged aperture? As if the vulva could not be enlarged, or relaxed by the tongue of the *cunnilingue* equally as much as by active cohabitation!

Tiberius Caesar in his retreat at Capri does not seem to have disdained the voluptuousness of the *cunnilingue*. Blasted by every other kind of abomination of what else is the Emperor accused in the Atellanian song (b), mentioned by Suetonius (*Tiberius*, 45), which was so much applauded:

"An old buck licking the vulvas of goats." but this of being a *cunnilingue*? Do you want to see Tiberius employed at his licking? Plate XXII, in *Moruments de la vie privée des douze Césars*, represents it.

(b) Atellanae—farces which, like the Commedia dell' Arte, had certain stock characters. They also contained puzzles to be explained, either in single lines or the plot.

So also Sextus Clodius (c), whom Cicero frequently reproaches with the impurity of his mouth and the obscenity of his tongue (*De Domo Sua* X, 25; XVIII, 47; *Pro Caelio* (XXXII, 78), appears to us to have been a *cunnilingue*. Hence, that hit of Cicero, in his *De Domo Sua* (ch. 18):

"My good Sextus, I ask your pardon, as you have lately become a good dialectician, you are licking your lips over your performances in this medium—as well as others."

Certainly if he licked more than his lips, he was bound to lick Clodia (d), the sister of Publius Clodius (e), (99) the wife of Metellus, the woman that was intimate with all the world. Cicero, *De Domo Sua* (XXXI, 83).

---

(99) But Clodia was something more than a sister to Publius Clodius; this would appear from the spirited pleasantry of Cicero, *Pro Caelio* (ch. 13):
"If there had not arisen differences between me and that lady's husband, ... brother, I should say; I always make that mistake."
(c) Sextus Clodius was a freedman of the Publius Clodius mentioned in the following paragraph.
(d) Clodia was the sister of Publius Clodius, with whom she had incestuous relations. She was the wife of Metellus Celer, whom she poisoned. She must have been a beautiful woman, for she is probably the Lesbia of the love poems of Catullus, and, prior to Cicero's break with Publius Clodius, Cicero's wife had reason to believe that Cicero was going to divorce her and marry Clodia.
(e) Publius Clodius Pulcher (died 52 BC) was of one of the oldest noble families in Rome, the Claudii. Both his father and brother became Consuls (both named Appius Claudius), but Publius voluntarily became a commoner so he could be elected Tribune in 58 BC. He was killed in 52 BC in a street fight.

"Ask Sextus Clodius as to this, cite him to appear; he is keeping quite in the background. But if you will have him looked for, he will be found near your sister (he is addressing Publius Clodius), lurking somewhere with his head low."

Pay attention, pray, to this expression: "the head low," it will soon reappear, when we speak of the Greeks.

The Greeks, in fact, felt no repugnance to the pleasure in question. *Epigrams* LXXIV, LXXV, and LXXVIa, in the *Aralecta* of Brunck (vol. III, p. 165) allude to this:

LXXIV.

"Homer taught you to use your voice (*enope*); but who taught you to use your tongue (*enope*) (in a slit)?"

The unknown poet plays upon the ambiguity of the word *enope*, which is used with respect to the tongue in an honest sense, when derived from *epo*, I speak, but as a vile usage when derived from *ope*, a slit.

LXXV.

"Avoid Alpheus' mouth, he loves Arethusa's bosom, plunging head-first into the salty sea."

In this epigram also the poet draws upon the ambiguity of the words mouth, bosom (bay), head-first, salty sea, which may refer to the river Alpheus in Arcadia and to Arethusa, a spring near Syracuse, but also to the mouth of a *cunnilingue*, that plunges in the vulva of a woman; not to mention yet another idea

connected with this, to which we shall return presently.

LXXVIa.

"Cheilon and *leichon* have the same letters, and
why? It is because Cheilon will lick things that are
like and unlike."

This mockery is addressed to the cunnilingue, Cheilon. The epigram tells him that he has somehow a
right of licking, as his name, composed of the same
letters as *leichon*, announces at once the licker,
whether he may lick the lips of a mouth, similar to his
own, or those of a vulva, which are very dissimilar.

The distich of Meleager (f) upon Phavorinus, published by Huschkius in his *Analecta critica* (p. 245),
seems to bear upon the same subject:

"You doubt whether Phavorinus does the thing.
Doubt no more; he told me himself he did,—*with his
own mouth.*"

As Martial uses often very happily the word *narrat*
(III, 84), when he speaks of the abuse of the tongue
for *fellation*, and Horace the same, so Meleager says
eipe (he told) of the man, who employs his licking the
vulva.

The following epigram of Ammianus (g), from the
Analecta of Brunck (vol. II, p. 386), is somewhat more
obscure:

_____
(f) Meleager (c140-70 BC), a Greek poet of mainly erotic
epigrams. This is Book XI, 223 in the Loeb Edition of the
Greek Anthology.
(g) Ammianus (2nd century AD). Except for his few
epigrams, nothing is known of him.

"It is not because you lick your pen that I dislike you; it's because you do so,—without a pen (h)."

The scholiast imagined the author wanted to upbraid a lazy pupil who passed his time sucking his pen, as do others biting their nails, and to scold him at the same time for sucking without a pen, meaning for being a *cunnilingue*. But it may be taken to refer, and I think with more reason, to a man who is in the habit of putting out his tongue for the obscene act of the *cunnilingue*, and who is so accustomed to it that he puts it out in the ordinary intercourse of life.

This monstrous practice was pushed to such lengths that, it is almost incredible, there were people who, not content to lick vulvas which were dry, did it when they were humid with the menses or any other secretion. Aristophanes says of Ariphrades, in the *Knights* (V. 1283-86):

"He is not only lewd; his fancy goes astray; he pollutes his tongue with shameful pleasures, licking up in his orgies the abominable dew, fouling his beard and tormenting women's privates."

Tormenting women's privates, licking the dew, staining the beard, there you have the man whom humid vulvas do not disgust! there you have a beard like that of the Ravola of Juvenal (IX, 4), "when he with wet beard rubs against the groin of Rhodope." However, not to be dogmatic, it may be admitted that Ravola's wet beard may have been intended as merely the wet hair of a fornicator's pubis. From the

(h) Book XI, 221 in the Loeb Edition of the Greek Anthology, substitutes sugarcane for pen. The Greek (Kalamos) and the Latin (Calamus) can be either a reed pen or a cane of sugar.

above passage of Aristophanes we may deduce surely
enough that the expression "working with the tongue,"
which he also uses, rather ambiguously, with respect
to the same Ariphrades, applies to a *cunnilingue*
rather than to a *fellator*. (*Wasps*, 1280-83):

"Then Ariphrades, the best endowed of all, of whom
his father said once, he never had a teacher, but
prompted by nature, of his own free will, learned how
to work his tongue, visiting every brothel!"

The same personage reappears in the *Peace* (885),
where he is described without any circumlocution as
imbibing the feminine secretion by way of a sauce:

"And throwing himself on her he will drink up all
her juice."

The Greeks however had in this kind of voluptuousness a host of imitators amongst the Romans. Mamercus Scaurus is known to us through Seneca (*De
Beneficiis*, IV, 31, 3), in this light:

"Did you not know when you appointed Mamercus
Scaurus as Consul, that he swallowed the menses of
his servant girls by the mouthful? Did he make a
secret of it? Did he pretend to be a blameless man?"

Similarly with Natalis (*Letter* LXXXVII, 16):

"Lately Natalis, that man with a tongue as malicious
as it is impure, in whose mouth women used to eject
their monthly purgation ..."

Both of them were consequently "imbibers of
menses," an appellation which, as we have seen in
chapter III, Galen applies to *cunnilingues*.

Now too, we can clearly understand the meaning of
Nicarchus' (i) epigram against Demonax, vol. III, p.

(i) Nicarchus (fl. 70 AD) about whom nothing is known.
This is Book XI, 329, in the Loeb Greek Anthology.

334 of Brunck's *Analecta*:

"Do not, Demonax, regard all things with downcast
head, and do not spoil your tongue with over-gratifica-
tion; the sow has threatening bristles. You live
amongst us, but you sleep in Phoenicia, and though no
son of Semele, you are thigh-reared. (j)."

He never looks up, exactly like the cinede Maternus
of Martial (I, 97); he gratifies his tongue, which likes
erection; whether the vulva be covered with hair or
depilated, he does not mind; during the day he lives in
Greece, but sleeps in Phoenicia, because he stains his
mouth with the monthly flux, which is, as every one
knows, of the color of Phoenician dye (100), viz., pur-

(j) Sow, here, means vulva. Dionysus (Bacchus) was the
son of Semele and Zeus. The child was born prematurely
and Zues sewed it up in his thigh until it was mature.
Phoinikes is Phoenicia, while *phoinikeos* is purple-red.
(100) Gonzalvo of Cordova, according to Luisa Sigea
(*Dialogue* VII), made similar jokes: "He also, I am sure, in
spite of his age, was a great tongue-player (linguist). A
pretty girl of some twenty years had to amuse him. When
he wanted to put his tongue to her *juste milieu*, he
declared he wanted to go to Liguria." He could play with
words upon the same matter, always implying the idea of
a humid vulva, saying that he was going to Phoenicia, or
to the Red Sea, or to the Salt Lake. You now understand
what is meant by the Salt Lake or Salt Sea, into which
Alpheus threw himself according to the epigram in the
Anthology. Nearly related to this are the *salgamas* of
Ausonius, of which we shall speak shortly, and the "onions
swimming in putrid brine," which the Baeticus of Martial
(III, 77) devours. As it was said of the fellators that they
"Phoenicianized," because they followed the example set
by the Phoenicians, so probably the same word was
applied to the *cunnilingues* as loving to swim in a certain
sea of Phoenician red; and, in fact, this was the case.
Hesychius: "Scylax, an erotic posture, like that assumed by

plish red; like another Bacchus, he draws his nourishment from a thigh (101). This scarcely needs an explanation. You can picture the *cunnilingue*, with his mouth glued between the thighs, at work.

This strange depravity was still in favor in succeeding centuries. Ausonius, in his *Epigrams* (k) CXX, CXXIII, CXXIV, CXXV, CXXVI, CXXVII, and CXXVIII, has bequeathed a very unenviable notoriety to the names of Castor and of Eunus:

Epigram CXX:

"When Castor (102) longed in vain to lick men's middles, but could take no one home with him he found means not to lose out on the groin altogether, fellator as he was; he started to lick his own wife's organs."

Phoenicianizers." The Phoenicians assumed a certain posture, called Scylax, or *the dog*. There could be nothing better for describing the depraved acction of a *cunnilingue* than this canine epithet with regard to the posture taken for irrumating or fellation; dogs are *cunnilingues*, as anybody knows, and have been so ever since that abominable adventures which their ambassadors met with. (Allusion to Phaedrus' fable).

(101) Ovid, *Metamorphoses* (III. 307-12):

". . . Mortal woman could not survive the celestial fire; she was consumed by her spouse's favors. The infant but half-formed is torn from the mother's womb, and, if we may believe the tale, is sewn still immature in the father's thigh, and there completes the period of gestation."

(102) This Castor is perhaps the same who, according to the statement of Ausonius (*Epigram in Professoribus Burdegalensibus*, XXII, 7) had published a book with the title *Cunctis de Regibus ambiguis*.

(k) These are LXXVIII, and LXXXII through LXXXVII in the Loeb Edition of Ausonius.

Epigrams CXXIII and CXXIV, both entitled *In Eunum liguritorem.*—On Eunus the Licker:

"Eunus, why do you pay court to Phyllis, the perfume seller? Men say your tongue knows her parts, but not your member! Mind you make no mistakes in the names of her scents and perfumes, and that Seplasia's atmosphere play you no tricks; think not costus and cysthus have the same odor,—that sardines and nard exhale the same savor."

"Poor Eunus! the things that he tastes and smells are very different; his mouth and his nose have tastes widely dissimilar!"

He says mockingly; think not the sundry wares in the shop of Phyllis your little perfume seller of Capua (Seplasia is in fact a street of the town of Capua where perfumes were sold), are all of the same odor and savor. The costus (103) does not smell like the cysthus (104), the nard (105) has a different flavor from the sardines,—a sort of little fish preserved in salt. By this salty condiment, Ausonius means to imply precisely the same as the author of the Greek epigram signifies, when he speaks of the Salt Sea, and which he himself has called *salgama*, meaning the secretion of the humid vulva. But Eunus shows no discrimination between what he licks and what he smells; the two

---

(103) Pliny, *Nat. Hist.* (XII, xxv, 41): "The costus-root has a burning taste and an exquisite smell; its berries are otherwise useless."

(104) The cysthus, Greek *kysthos*, is the private parts of a woman. Aristophanes, *Lysistrata* (1158): "And a more beautiful cysthus I never saw."

(105) Pliny, *Nat. Hist.* (XII, 12): "The leaves of the nard must be considered more minutely, for they are a principal ingredient in perfumery."

have nothing in common. He inhales perfumes which smell beautifully, and licks the vulva, which smells abominably. His nose obeys one law, his tongue another.

Epigram CXXV, directed against the same Eunus:

"The *salgamas* are no balmy odors; give place, all other perfumes. I would rather not smell at all, either good or bad."

Here again the poet plays with the words. The perfumes which Phyllis sells he calls balms, and *salgamas* those which her vulva exhales. Properly speaking, *salgamas* are roots and greens, which are preserved in salt for winter use, and the odor of which is not pleasant to everyone's nose. His saying that he would rather smell nothing at all than smell something bad is borrowed from Martial (VI, 55) against Coracinus, who was a *cunnilingue*):

"Rather than smell bad scents I would not smell at all."

Epigram CXXVI:

"Lais, Eros and Itys, CHiron and Eros, Itys once again,—if you write the names, and take the initial letters, they make a word, and that word is what you do, Eunus. What that word is and means, decency lets me not say in plain Latin."

The initial letters of the six Greek names from the word *leichei*, he licks. The phallic poet (*Priapeia,* LXVII) plays in the same way upon the word *paedicare* (to pedicate):

"Take the first syllable of *P*enelope; add to it the first of *D*ido; then to the first of *C*anis, append the first of *R*emus: what they make, I will do to you, thief, if I catch you in my garden. This is the penalty your crime will meet."

Ausonius plays on the words *doing* and *making*. The
initials of the Greek words *make* a word he cannot say
in Latin,—it is too indecent. Yet Eunus has no hesita-
tion in *doing* it,—putting it in action.

Epigram CXXVII:

"Eunus, when you lick the groin of your wife, she
being with child; 'tis because you would be ahead of
time in *teaching the tongues* to your babes yet unborn.

You seem, he says, to send out your tongue to meet
your unborn children, and fulfilling your duty as a
Grammarian, to teach them lessons of tongue, and the
interpretation of obscure terms (106). The Manneius of
Martial, whom we have spoken of previously, was also
in the habit of licking pregnant women's privates.

Epigram CXXVIII, entitled *On the same Eunus, the
Learned Licker*:

"Eunus, the little Syrian pedagogue, licker of pri-

------

(106) Quintilian, *Instit. orat.* (I, ch. 1): "He can learn the
interpretation of the occult languages, what the Greeks
call *glossas*." Alcuin, *Grammatica* (p. 2086) in Putschius'
Collection: "*Glossa* is the interpretation of a verb or a
noun; *e.g. catus* is the same thing as *doctus*." On this
occasion it may be permitted to the Director of the Court
Library at Coburg to state, that this library contains a
remarkable copy of the collection of Putschius, by the
hand of John Scheffer who died at Upsala in 1679,
beginning thus: "The notes to be found in this volume, on
the margins of books IV and V, of Priscian, have been
made after a very ancient and most beautifully written
manuscript, in which a number of traces of primitive Latin
orthography are found, as for instance: *dirivare*, for *deri-
vare*, *peneultimus* and *antepeneultimus* for *penultimus* and
antepenultimus, *Oratius* for *Horatius*, etc."

vates, Opican doctor ('tis Phyllis he owes his knowledge to), beholds the feminine engine in the fourfold
different fashions: Opening it triangularly, he makes it
the letter Delta (Δ); seeing the pair of folds side by
side along the valley of the thighs with the line in the
middle where the slit of the vagina opens, he says it is
a Psi (Ψ); in fact its shape is triple-cloven then. Then
when he has put his tongue in, it is a Labda (Λ),
and he makes out therein the true design of a Phi (Φ).
Why! ignoramus, do you think you see a Rho (Ρ)
written, where merely a long Iota (Ι) should be put?
Contemptible doctor, foul pedant, you deserve the
Tau (Τ) yourself; the crossed Theta (Θ) should by
rights be put against your name."

Ausonius calls Eunus an Opican, because these
filthy practices were, according to Festus, most common among the Osci or Opici. He then indulges in a
series of jests, or rather represents Eunus as doing so,
on the shape of the female organ (107). He says it

(107) As we are on the subject of the shape of the female
organ, it will not be amiss to enumerate in this place all
the various names by which it was known in Latin; the
greater part of them we have gathered from the treasure-
house of Luisa Sigea: The field, the ring, the furrow, the
cavern, the clitoris, the conch-shell, the cunnus, the little
boat, the cysthus, the pit, the garden, the between-thighs,
the barque, the swine, the wicket, the slit, the precipice,
the hole, the trench, the sheath, the virginal, the vulva.
And what should hinder us from giving at the same time
the names of the virile member: The armature of the belly,
the catapult, the tail, the stem, the parcel, the column, the
pole, the lance with balls, the amulet, the pike, the groin,
the hanger, the mentula, the mutinus, the muto, the nerve,
the virile sign, the stake, the peculia, the penis, the
stopper, the phallus, the javelin, the tree, the obelisk, the
shaft, the spectre, the seminal member, the awl, the bull,

seems to him either quadrangular, or triangular, in the
latter case corresponding to the Greek Δ (similarly
Aristophanes called it a Delta,—"their delta plucked
clean of hair," *Lysistrata*, 151), and also likens it to
the letter Ψ, owing to the folds which surround the
vulva on either side (108), and form the outer lips, the
lane in the middle being the opening of the vulva, and
so together from the trifid letter Ψ; in the *Techno-
paegnium*, (140), he calls it a three-pronged fork, the
slit being the middle and the lips the outer prongs.
Then he says that Eunus is a Labda when he is
licking, on account of the first letter of the word
leichein. All this is clear enough, and I do not understand how the very learned Vinet can complain of its
obscurity. Neither has it given me much trouble to
make out what Ausonius means by the letters Rho and
Iota. The solution seems to me to be as follows: "Do
not tell us, Eunus, that your pike in action resembles
the letter P of the Greeks, a letter which evidently
looks like a lance with balls; in your amorous diver-
sions you use no other lance than your tongue, which,
as you will not deny, looks more like a javelin without
balls, something like the letter Iota; you cannot deceive me, who well know that you would rather be

---

the dart, the ballista, the beam, the thyrsus, the vessel, the
little vessel, the vein, the private, the verpa and verpus,
the verge, the plowshare. Here you have more than
enough.

(108) *Altrinsecus*, in Ausonius, is equivalent to *utrinsecus*,
meaning, from either side. Lactantius employs that word
in *De Opificio Dei* (ch. 8): "It is incredible how the fact of
their being double (the ears) adds to their beauty, as much
on account of the symmetry thus produced, as because the
sounds which arise on all sides can more easily be received
on both sides (*altrinsecus*)."

taken for a fornicator than for a *cunnilingue*, like that
Gargilius, of whom Martial (III, 96) says:

"You do not enter, only lick my mistress; yet you
boast yourself adulterer and copulator!"

Lastly and finally by the Tau he threatens his man
with the gallows, and by the Theta with death. Of this
there can be little doubt; it is a proved fact that the
letter Theta, the initial of the word *thanatos* (death),
signified with the Greeks condemnation to death (109).
With regard to Tau, there is room for doubt; instead
of Tau some of the copies of Ausonius give 8, and
although this sign may, according to Scaliger, very
well signify the rope for hanging, the difficulty I feel is
this, that a composite letter, a small letter, an abbre-
viation of doubtful antiquity, thus placed amonst simple, capital, unabbreviated letters, seems to come in
very inappropriately. It may be that Ausonius original-
ly wrote *tau*; then *t* having been left out by an
inadevertence of the copyist, the *au* might easily have
been turned into *ou*. (1). The Tau, as the reader will
see at once, represents a gallows. Tertullian, *Adversus
Marcionem*: "This letter Tau of the Greeks is with us
the T, a sort of cross."

As was the case with irrumation, so with even more
reason the licking of women's privates was particularly adopted by old men, whose tool will not raise its
head (110). Luisa Sigea, *Dialogue* VII, says: "He
(Gonzalvo of Cordova), was likewise a mighty *cunni-*

---

(1) It was customary to print the Greek *ou* with the *u* over
the *o*(8).
(109) Persius (IV, 13): "And you may mark the crime with
a black Theta." See also Martial (VII, 37).
(110) I say it was adopted by them particularly; that there
were also young men, who by a singular depravity licked
the vulvas they might have entered legitimately, Martial
tells us (XI, 85):

lingue by reason of his great age."

Martial (XI, 47):

"Why does Blatara lick? because he cannot manage otherwise."

The same author (VI, 26):

"Sotades has lost the power of stiffening; so licks."

And again (XII, 87):

"Thirty young boys you have at command, and as many girls; yet you have only one member, and that will not rise. What then will you do?"

Lick, no doubt, as we are told Linus did, in *Epigr.*, (XI, 25):

"This too frisky mentula, Linus, so well known to girls in plenty, will no longer stand; so mind your tongue."

Sextillus (Martial, II, 28), was in all probability also a *cunnilingue*:

"Have your laugh at those, Sextillus, that call you cinede, and show them your middle finger (111). You

---

"An evil star, Zoilus, has struck your tongue of a sudden, even while licking a vulva. Of a surety, Zoilus, you must now use your member."

(111) When the middle finger is pointing, the other fingers are turned inside, representing thus a mentula with its accessories; for which reason it was thus pointedly shown to cinedes (the Greeks expressed this in a single word: *skimalizein*), either by way of invitation or to tease them. Martial (I, 93): "Cestus has often complained to me Mamurianus, that you tease him with your finger." It was also pointed at people held in contempt. The same author (VI, 70):

"He points with the finger and that the impudent finger" (that is: Martianus, who is never ill, does so to the doctors). Thence this unlucky finger had the epithet "infamous." Persius says, without any obscene afterthought (II, 31-4): "The grandmother cleanses the babe with the infamous (middle) finger."

are not, Sextillus, a pedicon, nor yet a fornicator, nor
does Vetustilla's burning mouth tempt you.—You are
none of these, I allow, Sextillus; then what are you? I
know not, but remember! there are two sorts yet."

Two sorts are still left for Sextillus, to suck the virile
member and to lick the vulva, while he is neither a
fornicator, nor a cinede, nor a pedicon, nor an irrumator. Which did he choose to be? This we are not told.
Eunuchs, just as impotent as aged men, adopt the
practice for the same reason (112). Gregory Nazianzen

---

(112) Nevertheless, eunuchs who have been deprived of
their testicles, but not of their mentula, are by no means
wanting in lubricity; they can do the business without any
danger for a woman, inasmuch as they cannot generate
children. The Roman matrons were well aware of the fact;
Martial (VI, 67):
"You ask me, Pannicus, why Gallia keeps so many eunuchs; she loves to be enjoyed, but wants no children."
Juvenal (VI, 365-67):
"There are women who like feeble eunuchs, and kisses
that are ever harmless, and the absence, nay! the impossi-
bility, of a beard, for they need use no abortive."
St. Jerome, in the *Life of Hilarion*: "A steward with curled
locks, castrated for the sake of longer pleasure and perfect
safety . . ." To make more sure of their enjoyment, experienced dames did not allow the testicles of their eunuchs to
be cut off until the member had attained full proportions,
apprehensive that it might remain puny and inactive if the
operation were made earlier. They wanted their eunuchs
well furnished, capable of challenging Priapus himself. By
such they liked to be worked, being sure of not becoming
pregnant.
Juvenal (VI, 367-77):
"With those however is love's pleasure most exquisite,
whose testicles, when they are lusty and fully matured, are
delivered to the surgeons, the pubis being already black
with hair. The organs are spared till they are full and
ready; then at last, when they have reached two pounds in
weight, Heliodorus cuts them, to the prejudice of the

(m) says in his funeral sermon on Basil the Great:

"They of the gynaeceum (n), those men, who amongst women are men, and amongst men women; who have nothing virile about them but their impiety; those who cannot give themselves up to voluptuousness in the natural way, have recourse to their tongue as their only alternative."

The *cunnilingues* exhaled an evil smell from the mouth, and their kisses were as much shunned as those of *fellators*. Martial (XII, 86):

"You say the mouths of pedicons smell badly; if this is true, Fabullus, as you say, tell me! what think you of the breath of *cunnilingues*?"

And the same (XII, 59):

"The neighbors kiss you every one, from the bearded cowherd, whose kisses have flavor of the he-goat, down to the *fellator* and the *cunnilingue* fresh from his business."

Cunnilingues and *fellators* are compared to he-goats by Catullus (XXXVII, 3-5), on account of their fetid breath:

"Think you, you alone have members, that you alone are entitled to satisfy women, and may consider all other men he-goats?"

---

barber. The observed of all observers, stared at by all, see him enter the baths and challenge the god of vineyard and garden, castrated thus by his lady's order. He may sleep now with his mistress; still beware, Posthumus, how you trust him with your Bromius, now fully developed and ready for the razor."

(m) St. Gregory of Nazianzus (c329-389), Patriarch of Constantinople and vigorous defender of orthodox Christianity. He left many orations, much poetry and other works.

(n) Gynaeceum is the women's quarters of a Greek house.

Do not suppose for a moment that Catullus is speaking here of castrated he-goats, which would be against the sense of the word, one invariably used to designate he-goats. The sense is the same, but got at in another way. He says: "Do you believe that you alone have members fit to do the girls' business? that all the others betray by their goatish breath their vile trade as *cunnilingues* or *fellators*, and consequently the inertness of their mentulas, their feebleness, their inability for erection? You will better appreciate the sting of the Atellane verse respecting Tiberius Caesar: "An old buck licking the vulvas of goats."

It was thought better to be taken for a fornicator than for a *cunnilingue*; in the first place, because your friends would not kiss you. Martial (VII, 95):

"I had rather confront a hundred *cunnilingues*."

Suetonius, *De Illustribus Grammaticis* (23):

"He (Remmius Palaemon) was passionately fond of women, so much so as to prostitute his mouth to please them, and it is said that he was one day rebuked in the following way by a man, who in the throng could not contrive to avoid one of his kisses: 'Master,' he said, 'when you see a man in a hurry to get away, do you always try to lick him off?'"

In the second place for fear of scaring away your guests. Aristophanes says of Ariphrades, in the *Knights* (1288-89):

"Whoever does not execrate that man, may he never drink from the same cup with us."

Lastly, for fear of letting it be plainly known how shrunken one was, and how miserable one's member. Martial (III, 96):

"You lick my mistress, but you do not enter her; yet you boast yourself adulterer and copulator!"

Hence the *cunnilingues* took no less care than the *fellators* to hide the fetidness of their breath by means of essences and perfumes. Martial (VI, 55):

"Always scented with cassia and cinnamon, and your skin darkened with perfumes from the Phoenix' (o), you reek of the leaden jars of Nicerotus' shop. You mock at us, Coracinus, because we are unscented. Rather than smell sweet like you, I'd not smell at all."

To remove every doubt as to Coracinus being a *fellator* or a *cunnilingue*, we will quote *Epigr.*, IV, 43, where he is expressly called a *cunnilingue*:

"I did not say you are a cinede, Coracinus; I am not so rash and reckless. What I did say is a light, insignificant matter, one perfectly well known, that you will not deny yourself,—I said, Coracinus, you are a *cunnilingue.*"

It was believed that Venus revenged injuries done to herself or to hers, not only by condemning the guilty to submit to be the passive party, but by turning them into *cunnilingues.* Hence the pathic tastes of Philoctetes:

"Of the sort the loneliness of Lemnos taught the heir of Hercules."

To use the very words of Ausonius (*Epigr.*, LXXI); and by inflicting these tastes Venus is said to have avenged the wounds of Paris. Martial (II, 84):

"The son of Poeas was effeminate and prone to man-love; thus they say did Venus avenge Paris' wounds."

In the same epigram Martial taunts Sertorius on being a *cunnilingue*, giving as a possible reason his having killed Eryx, the son of Venus:

(o) For the meaning of Phoenix, see note j, this chapter.

"Why does the Sicilian lick women's private; because,
Rufus, it would seem it was he killed Eyrx."

Cunnilingues appear to have been generally pale-
faced; it is for medical men to say why. This may help
you to discern the salt in Martial's epigram on Charinus (I, 78):

"Charinus is well and strong, and still he is pale;
Charinus drinks with moderation, and still he is pale;
Charinus digests well, and still he is pale;
Charinus loves the open air and sun, and still he is
pale;
Charinus dyes his skin, and still he is pale;
Charinus licks a woman's privates, and still pale is
he."

That is to say, amongst the causes that should
prevent paleness the one last enumerated is the veritable cause of his paleness. *Fellators* would also seem to
have had pale faces. Catullus (LXXX):

"How is it, Gellius, that those rosy lips of yours
grow whiter than the winter's snow, when at morn you
leave your house, and the eighth hour calls you from
your long-protracted soft repose? I know not what to
think. Can it be true what rumor whispers, that you
devour the middle parts of men? This at any rate is
evidenced by wretched Virro's sunken flanks and your
own lips masked with the milky juice sucked from
him."

The withered flanks are those of Virro, the *irrumator*, the lips those of Gellius; the passage is somewhat
ambiguous, and only thus to be explained. One Virro,
accustomed to take the passive part, has been already
mentioned by us, in quoting Juvenal (IX, 35). I do not

know whether he is the same one:

"Though Virro has caught sight of you all naked with lips that water."

Pathics too, no less than *fellators*, appear to have had pallid faces. Juvenal (II, 50):

"Hispo submits to young men; he is pale with either kind of infamy."

He served as *patient* to young men, and was moreover a *fellator*, as is shown by the difference which the poet institutes between him and women, who do not lick each other's secret parts (II, 49):

"Media does not lick Cluvia, nor Flora, Catulla."

Women, in fact, are rarely *cunnilingues*, although there *are* examples. Martial only mentions one woman as belonging to that category; we shall come across her again in the next chapter.

OF TRIBADS

CHAPTER SIX

OF TRIBADS

The tribads, also called frictionists (113), from the
Greek *tribo*, I rub, are women, with whom that part of
the genital apparatus which is called the clitoris,
attains such proportions, that they can use it as a
mentula, either for fornication or pedication. The clitoris (114), which is a very sensitive caruncle (a small
fleshy cone), capable of movement and resembling the
verge, gets into erection with all women, not only

(113) They were also called *hetairistriai*:—Hesychius: "Hetairistriai tribads"—and likewise *dietairistriai*, according to
the same author: "Dietairistriai, women who go after prostitutes (hetairai) for carnal intercourse, just as men do; same
as tribads."
(114) Luisa Sigea, *Dialogue* III: "But I forgot (Tullia
speaking) to tell you of the clitoris. This is a membranous
body, situated at the bottom of the pubis, and representing
in a reduced form the virile verge. As is the case with the
verge, the amorous desire excites it to erection, and in
certain women of an ardent temperament it inflames them
with pruriency to such a degree that by the mere caressing
of it with the hand they very often discharge their fluid
without the help of a rider at all."

during the coitus, the delights of which it is said to enhance immensely by increased titillation, but also in consequence of mere amorous longing; with tribads, either by a freak of nature or in consequence of frequent use, it attains immoderate dimensions (115).

---

(115) If that woman whom Plater saw, according to Venette in his *Tableau de l'amour conjugal* (vol. I, chap. 1, 3), was not a tribad, she might well have been one; her clitoris, which with other women attains in its utmost erection the length of the half of the little finger or thereabouts, was as long as the neck of a goose. Is it surprising that women furnished with such an implement should wish to get rid of it? Amputation is however dangerous. Plater did not venture to finish an amputation which he had commenced, and Rodohamides, an Egyptian physician of the 11th century, had not courage to even undertake one, although commanded by a Queen to perform the operation (Venette, IV, 2). Those whom Adramytes, the King of the Lydians, ordered to castrate women, were they more courageous? Athenaeus (XII, 515): "Xanthus states in the second book of his *Lydian History* that Adramytes, King of the Lydians, was the first to have women castrated and employ them as eunuchs." However that may be, these female eunuchs have very much exercised the commentators. Some suppose that straps and buckles did in their case the same service as the chastity-belts, which, it is said, Spaniards and Italians to this day compel their wives to wear if they think they have reason to be jealous; others believe that it was a question of suture, as is the case with the natives of Angola and the Congo, who stitch the vulvas of young girls for the protection of their maidenheads; but I believe that nobody knows anything certain in this respect. Nor does it appear that these women had to submit to an operation, which is certainly practised upon the young girls by the Arabs, Copts, Ethiopians, in some parts of Persia and Nigera, and which consists in cutting off the prepuce of the clitoris; this is proved by abundant evidence, and reported in the *Allgemeine Encyklopaedie* of Ersch and Gruber under the

The tribad can get it in erection, enter a vulva or
anus, enjoy a delicious voluptuousness, and procure if
not a complete realisation of cohabitation, at least
something very near to it, to the woman who plays the
passive part. What more is there to say? She plays the
man's part with the omission of the ejaculation of the
semen, not that this sort of coitus is an altogether dry

---

word: *"Beschneidung"* (Circumcision); how indeed could
Athenaeus describe as *Eunuchize* that which is calculated
to increase the fecundity of women. I thought first that
these women were tribads changed into eunuchs by the
removal of their immoderately large clitoris; I am now
inclined to believe that the King caused that to be done to
these women, which according to Aristotle (*Nat. Hist.*, IX,
50), was done to sows: "Sows are castrated, so that they
shall no longer desire the coitus, and get quickly fattened.
They are castrated, suspended by their hind legs, after
fasting two days, by an incision in that place where with a
man the testicles are situated, in fact in the female
matrix." Pliny, *Nat. Hist.* (VIII, lxxvii, 209): "Sows are
castrated in the same way as female camels, after a fast of
two days, suspended by their hind legs, by an incision in
the vulva; they thus fatten much quicker." Columella (VII,
IX. 5): "Sows also are castrated by incision in the womb;
the wounds close up as a result of scarring over, and they
cannot conceive any more." This practice has by no means
disappeared; Schneider notes it in the passage of Columella: sows, cows, mares, sheep, are still castrated by excising
their ovaries. Why should we not believe that Adramytes
wanted the same process to be applied to the fair sex, in
order to make women sterile? However the ancient Egyptians, who (see Strabo, book XVII, p. 824) undoubtedly
circumcised themselves, and also their women, appear to
me to have had in view not so much ovariotomy as the
circumcision of the prepuce of the clitoris, a practice still
in use with them, as stated above; cutting the female parts
being thus something like circumcision, it is to be assumed
that a similar operation was intended rather than any other
one.

affair, as women are in the habit of emitting their
liquid during the joys of love (116).

---

(116) Let us consult again Luisa Sigea (*Dialogue* III): "It
has happened sometimes to myself (Tullia), when Callias
tries on me his lubricities, when he tickles me and excites
me, then I sometimes water his too libertine hands with an
abundant dew from my pleasure grounds. And that gives
him an opportunity for letting off a whole sheaf of sar-
casms and jokes. But what can I do? I begin to laugh, and
so does he; I tell him he is too impudent, he tells me I am
too lewd; we call each other names right and left, and in
the midst of our mutual recrimination he will throw
himself upon me, turn me on my back, and force me to
submit to his assault, saying he will give me his dewdrops
for those he has drawn from me, so that I may not be a
loser." Farther on (*Dialogue* IV): "Callias, pressing me
more closely to him, buried his weapon deeper into my
belly, almost as though he were trying to get himself in
altogether. Soon a delicious stream spurted into me, and at
the same time I felt my liquid boiling over, causing me
such delight that I forgot all reticence, and myself excited
Callias more and more, pressing him against me and
begging him to quicken his pace. Thus we expired both
together with our muscles relaxing at one and the same
instant." You will understand by this the meaning of the
epigram of Sosipator in the *Analecta* of Brunck (I, p. 504):
"Until the white liquor ran over with both of them, and
Doris unwound her wearied limbs."
Reiske thought the "white liquor" in this passage meant
drops of perspiration. Nonsense! it means the virus secreted by both sexes, and liberated in the last spasms of
lust. Luisa Sigea (*Dialogue* IV): "As I finished speaking" (it
is still Tullia who speaks), "he got upon me, and collecting
all his strength he pushed the arrow into me, he filled my
womb with his fecundating dew, and I also shed the
rivulet of white liquid. Incapable of enduring any longer
so intense a voluptuous feeling, we sank back exhausted in
each other's arms." We have quoted besides on different
occasions extracts from the rich treasures of Luisa Sigea on
this subject.

This depravity of voluptuousness, whether caused
by the warmth of the climate, or by a peculiarity of
the soil or waters, or other reasons unknown to us, was
especially common with the women of Lesbos; this is
attested by all the old writers. Lucian, in his *Dialogues of Courtesans*, (No. V; Works, vol. VII, p. 349):
"This is one of those tribads, as they are to be found in
Lesbos, who will have nothing to do with men, and do
the men's business with women." If such things were
an every day occurrence with the Lesbian women, we
must believe that they were pushed to them by natural instigation (117), and to allay an intolerable pruriency. Who has not heard of that most celebrated
Queen of all tribads, Sappho, (a) herself a Lesbian?
Some authors, Maximus of Tyre (b), the first amongst
them, have with the best intention tried to exonerate
her from this infamous vice; but hear her in Ovid (and
he represents the Ancients in sentiment and feeling),
repudiating her would be apologists, *Heroides* (XV,
15-20):

"Neither the maidens of Pyrrha, nor those of Methymna (118), nor all the host of Lesbian beauties please

---

(117) Women, whose clitoris is too prominent, are thus
prevented from having intercourse with men, so that when
they are seized with amorous designs they cannot well find
any other way of satisfying their desires than by playing
tribadism. (Venette, IV, ii, 4).
(a) Sappho of Lesbos (c630-c570 BC), by some considered
the greatest of poets. Some consider her chaste and above
reproach, others view her as licentious. There is no evidence, only hearsay, for either view.
(b) Maximus of Tyre (late 2nd century BC), the Greek
author of rhetorical essays on philosophical subjects.
(118) Pyrrha and Methymna are towns in Lesbos. Pompon-

me. Vile to me seems Anactoria, vile the fair Cydno,
Atthis is no more so dear to my eyes as once she was,
nor yet a hundred others I loved not innocently (119).
Villain! yours is now what belonged to many
women . . ."
and verse 201:

"Lesbian women, beloved, who made me infamous!"

Sappho speaks first in general of those who have
submitted to her caresses, the maidens of Pyrrha and
Methymna; then she mentions by name Anactoria,
Cydno and Atthis,—to whom Suidas adds Telesippa
and Megara:

"Her favorites, whom she loved well, were three in
number, Atthis, Telesippa, Megara, and for those she
burned in impure passion."

These passages from the Ancients are clear enough,
and do not admit of any doubt; they even assist us in
explaining other sentences, which otherwise seem obscure or ambiguous; for instance the "masculine Sappho" of Horace (*Epistles* I, xix, 28); "complaining
against the maids of her country" (*Odes*, II, xii, 25);

---

ius Mela (c) (II, 7): "In the Troad is Lesbos, and in Lesbos
there were formerly five cities, viz.: Antissa, Pyrrha, Ere-
sos, Methymna, Mytilene."

(119) Not innocently, or rather, "not without crime;" some
read "which I loved not without crime," others, "which I
loved here without crime," but the difference is not great.
If you prefer "which I loved here," the excuse itself is a
confession. All we want is the admission that the tribad
tastes of Sappho are no modern invention, but originated,
how we know not, and prevailed in very early times. The
love of woman for woman was never known under any
other name than the notorious one of tribadism.

(c) Pomponius Mela of Spain (fl. 40 AD). wrote *De
Chorographia*, a description of the known world.

also Ovid, (*Art of Love,* III, 331):

"Sappho should be well known too; what more wanton than she?"

Tristia (II, 365):

"What was the lore Lesbian Sappho taught, but to love maids?"

and, Martial (VII, 69) (120):

"Sappho, the amorous, praised our poetess; the latter was more pure, the former not more perfect in art."

Lucian's witty and licentious pen has made famous another tribad, Megilla, in a previously quoted Dialogue. This Dialogue is not outrageously obscene, for it breaks off just at the moment when things would have had to be said very plainly; nevertheless, the virginal modesty of our Wieland has not dared to translate it into German. The philosopher of Samosata (Lucian) brings Leaena upon the scene, and makes her disclose by what artifices Megilla gained her consent. Leaena asks Megilla:

"'Are you then made like a man, and do with Demonassa (whom Megilla used after the manner of tribads), as men do?' 'I have not got exactly all that, my Leaena,' answers Megilla, 'but I am not entirely without it. However, you will see me at work, and in a very pleasant manner. I have been born like all of you, but I have the tastes, the desires and something else of a man. Let me do it to you, if you do not believe me, and you will see that I have everything that men have. Give me leave to work you, and you will see.' Leaena confesses that she at last consented, moved by her

_____

(120) See whether it is with good reason or not that the succeeding *Epigram* (No. 70) calls Philaenis the tribad of tribads.

solicitations and promises, and no doubt also by the
novelty of the thing. 'I let her have her way,' she says,
'yielding to her entreaties, seconded by a magnificent
necklet and a robe of fine linen. I took her in my arms
like a man; she went to work caressing me, panting
with excitement and evidently experiencing the extreme of pleasure.' Clonarion asks her inquisitively:
'But what did she do to you Leaena, and how did she
manage?' But Leaena eludes the question. 'Do not ask
me anything more; these are nasty doings; by Urania,
I shall not breathe a word more!' she answers," to the
great regret of the reader who would like to penetrate
further this mystery.

Amongst the tribads is still to be named Philaenis,
the same, no doubt, who according to Lucian
(*Amores*, ch. 28,—Works vol. V, p. 88), wrote about
erotic postures: "Let our women's apartments be filled
by women like Philaenis, dishonored by androgynic
(121) loves!—Sophoclidisca in Plautus, to whom Paeg-

---

(121) To make yourselves quite sure about what the author
means by androgynic loves, look at the passage as a whole:
"Come, you man of the new age, you law-giver of unknown amours, if you open out new ways to the lubricity of
men, you may grant to the women equal licence. Let them
cohabit together as the men do; let woman lie with
woman, and simulate with their lascivious organs conjunctions, sterile though they be, as man lies with man! Let the
word one hears so very rarely, and which I am ashamed to
pronounce, let the lubricity of our tribads triumph without
blushing." Observe in the first place how tribads were
seldom spoken of, and that they kept themselves in the
dark; in the second place how the immoderate clitoris of
the tribad is said to simulate lascivious organs in conjunction. Seneca (*Controversia*, II) in a similar sense, calls such
a monstrosity *andra proserraphthenta,* an *artificial man;*
lastly the epithet "sterile" is applied to the clitoris, and
points to the dry unproductiveness of the tribadic coitus.

nion says: "Do not caress me, subagitatrix!" (*Persia*,
Act II, sc. 2, 45);—and Folia of Ariminum, who according to Horace (*Epodes*, V, 41) was "of masculine
lubricity." However writers as a rule touch upon these
points more lightly than is agreeable to the curiosity
of the reader. For the same reason the too great
reserve of Seneca (*Controversia*, II) is to be regretted,
where he says at the end:

"Hybreas having to plead in favor of a man who
had surprised and killed a tribad, described the grief
of the husband; on such a subject one must not ask for
a too particular investigation."

Much more complete, full and explicit is our good
friend of Bilbilis (Martial). Hear him! he is disclosing
the tribadic doings of Bassa, so clearly that it could
not be done better (I, 91):

"As no one, Bassa, ever saw you go with men; as
rumor never assigned you a lover, as every office
about you was fulfilled by a troop of women, no man
ever coming nigh you, you seemed to us, I admit a
very Lucretia. But, oh! shame on you, Bassa, you were
a fornicator all the time! You dare to conjoin the
private parts of two women together, and your monstrous organ of love feigns the absent male. You have
contrived a miracle to match the Theban riddle: that
where no man is, there adultery should be!"

Surely it is clear enough what Bassa did, in conjoin-
ing the privates of two women together. By no means!
There are expounders, and very good ones too, who
have quite misunderstood this very easy passage, and
have imagined that Bassa misused women by introducing into their vagina a leather contrivance, an
olisbos, a dildo; we shall speak at the end of this

chapter of this kind of pleasure, but it was quite
unknown to Bassa, who simulated the man in her own
person.

Nothing could be more monstrous than the libertine
passion of Philaenis; she did not content herself with
introducing her stiff clitoris in the vulva of tribads—
Martial (VII, 70):

"Tribad of tribads, you, Philaenis, you are well
justified in calling her your mistress whom you work;"

—or in those of other young girls, and to get a
dozen of them under her in a day; but she even
pedicated boys. Martial (VII, 67):

Philaenis the tribad pedicates boys (122) and stiffer
than a man, in one day works eleven girls."

In order to leave nothing untasted in the way of
virile lusts she was also a *cunnilingue*; same epigram,
at the end:

"After all that, when she is in good feather,—she
does not suck, that is too feminine; she devours right
out girls' middle parts. May all the gods confound
you, Philaenis, who think it manly work to lick the
vulva."

Philaenis, when overmuch in rut, caused herself also

_____
(122) Instead of "pedicating boys," Martial might have
said, if the metre had allowed it, entering boys." Seneca's
expression (*Letter* XCV, 21) "*viros ineunt*," which was a
source of infinite trouble to the great Justus Lipsius,
signifies nothing else: "The women will contest for the
crown of lubricity with the men. May the gods confound
them! one of their refined lubricities reverses the laws of
Nature: they have connection with men!" There you have
in plain words the turpitude which Justus Lipsius considered worthy of the infernal regions: tribads pedicating.

to be served by *cunnilingues*; this is clear enough from
Marital (CIX, 41):

"When Diodorus, wanting the Tarpeian crowns, left
Pharos behind and sailed for Rome, Philaenis vowed
that to celebrate her mate's return, an innocent maid
should lick her, such an one as the chaste Sabine
women still cherish."

She vowed if her husband returned, she'd have her
vulva licked by a young girl well-known for her
innocence and chastity; to have it done by prostitutes
was for Philaenis nothing new; she wanted on that
occasion to experiment with a virgin, exactly like men,
who always want something new and strange to spur
their lust. How rare it was for women to use other
women for that purpose appears from Juvenal (II,
47-49):

" ... There will no other instance be found so
abominable in our sex; Media does not lick Cluvia, nor
Flora, Catulla."

But what could you find stronger, more energetic
and plainer to enlighten the reader completely on this
subject than the following verses in *Satire* VI
(308-333), where Juvenal's ire against the tribadic
orgies in Rome breaks out in words of fire?

"At night they stop their litters here, make water
here, and flood with long syphons the Goddess' statue,
and ride turn and turn about and go through the
motions under the eye of the conscious moon; then
they make for home. When the morning light returns,
you walk through your wife's urine, to visit your great
friends. Known are the secret rites of the *Bona Dea*,
when the flute excites their wanton loins, when drunk
with music and with wine they rush along, whirling

their locks and howling, these Maenads of Priapus!
How they yearn for instant copulation! how their
voice trembles with passionate longing! what floods of
old wine gush down their dripping thighs! A prize is
offered, and Laufeia challenges the brothel-master's
girls, and wins the first place for nimble hips; while
herself is mad for the pleasure Medullina's artful
movements give her. Amongst these dames merit carries off the palm from noble blood. There nothing
must be feigned, all must be done in very truth and
deed,—enough to set on fire, however, chilled with
age, Laomedon's son and old Nestor with his rupture!
Then is seen mere lust that will brook not a moment's
more delay, woman in her bare brutality, while from
every corner of the subterranean hall rises the reiter-
ated cry: 'The hour is come, admit the men.' Is the
lover asleep? she bids the first young man at hand to
snatch up his hood and come at once: Is none to be
found? resort is had to slaves. No hope of slaves? a
water-carrier will be hired to come. If he comes not,
and men there are none, she will not wait an instant
more but offer her buttocks to a young ass to mount
her from behind."

The tribadic orgies were divided into two kinds; in
one of them the Roman dames, giving free course to
their lust, defiled the altar of chastity; in the other
they celebrated the mysteries of the *Bona Dea* (d).
You see in the first place the tribads go at night in
litters to the altar of chastity, there pass their water
(123) against the statue of the Goddess, and having

_____

(123) When women are in rut they pass their water, nature
wills it so. Juvenal (VI, 63-65): "Let lewd Bathyllus dance
the pantomime of Leda:" (representing Leda receiving

perhaps spurted their urine up to her face (124) they
at all events wet the area all about, (their husbands
walking right through it in the morning, when they go
to see their patrons), and then they ride or allow
themselves to be ridden alternately; here we have
more than one Philaenis, tribad of tribads! Other
ladies go to celebrate the mysteries of the *Bona Dea*,

_____

Jupiter in a dance with wanton gestures): "Tuscia cannot
command her bladder, Appula is sighing as if in amorous
trance ..."
The same (XI, 166-68):
"The other sex however feels more pleasure, is aroused
much more, and lets the water off, excited through eyes
and ears."
(What Juvenal says here as to this greater enjoyment on
the part of the opposite sex is connected with his general
opinion that women experience more pleasure in Love
than men do. So his words in VI, 254: "For how
insignificant is our pleasure!" Tiresias, called upon to
arbitrate on this point in Lucian [*Amores*, p. 85], declared
women's enjoyment to be double that of men: "Unless
indeed we are to agree with Tiresias' arbitament, that the
woman's pleasure is twice that of the man.").
Martial (XI, 16):
"How often will your rigid nerve lift up your tunic, though
you be as stern as Curius or Fabricius! You too have to
read our pages, be they ever so lascivious, young maiden,
though you hail from Padua."
(124) There is some ambiguity about the "long syphons."
They are rivulets of urine near the statue, or perhaps
Juvenal means, to use the expression of Grange, "Urine
spurted right up into the Goddess' face, which may be
done by impudent women compressing with the hands
their parts, and thus retaining for some time the water;
thus collected it will spurt out with greater force."
(d) Bona Dea, "The Good Goddess," was the goddess of
chastity and of fruitfulness in women. Her rites were
celebrated on the night of May 3 and men were excluded.

well known to the public since the adventures of
Clodius (e) (125). You observe them rousing themselves with the sounds of flutes and trumpets, as also
with the fumes of wine, to undergo valiantly the jousts
of mutual love; you see their amorous frenzy, their
hair flying in the wind; you note their sighs of longing,
and how they pass water with excitement. A prize is
set, as in the feast of Pope Alexander VI, to be given
to the most intrepid tribad: Laufeia calls upon the
brothel-girls to let her ride them, and carries off the
crown (126); there is none there of better heart than
Medullina, expert in plying her loins and buttocks;
there all etiquette ceases, mistresses and servants alike
contest for the palm of obscenity; there is no sham, all
is tribadic reality (127); but, after all, finally nature got

----

(e) Publius Clodius Pulcher (see note e, ch. V) caused a
great scandal when discovered at the mysteries of Bona
Dea disguised as a woman.
(125) Juvenal (335-339):
"But all the Moors and Indians well know the flute-girl
who showed a bigger penis than great Caesar's two anti-
Catos in that place from which a rat will fly, conscious of
possessing testicles . . ."
(126) The "nimble hips" are those of the tribad, who is
riding another in the posture of Apuleius' Fotis (Metamorph., II, 20), when she gratified Lucias with the joys of
a superincumbent Venus.
(127) All this was actually represented in Paris, 1791, on
the stage of a theatre, where according to the author of
the Gynaeology (III, 423), a man completely naked had
connection with a woman as naked as himself, both
representing savages, accompanied by the plaudits of both
sexes. There is however nothing new under the sun. With
the Romans it had long been customary, after the public
games were finished, to bring prostitutes into the arena,
and set them to work, so that the spectators might have an

the upper hand again, the tribad disappeared, and the
woman became again a woman, leaving alone tribadism, as a phantom only of pleasure, and not satisfying them; from all parts a cry is raised: "Now is the
time for the men to come in: go and find young men;
if you cannot find any, then slaves will do; if they are
lacking, bring the first men you can find in the
streets." And if all fails, in their shameless wantonness,
they will offer their buttocks to an ass (128). On the

opportunity to perform what they had been looking at
with greedy eyes; a herald proclaimed what was to come.
Tertullian, *De Spectaculis* (ch. 17): "Prostitutes, the vic-
tims of public incontinence, are brought upon the stage,
shamefaced with respect to the women only; to the men
they were known; they are exposed to the laughter of all,
high and low; their dewellings their prices, even their
recommendations were proclaimed by the crier." Isidorus,
(f) *Origines*, (XVIII, 42): "The theatre is like a brothel;
when the games are over, public women are prostituted
there." The rape of the Sabines described in Livy (g) (II,
18) would seem to have been a not dissimilar form of
amusement: "In this year young Sabines in Rome having,
in the midst of the games, abducted some prostitutes, the
tumult ensuing thereupon degenerated into a riot, in fact
nearly into a battle."
(128) Observe the subtlety of the expression adopted by
the poet: "offers her buttocks to an ass to get on them."
Juvenal knows that a woman has no chance to have an
ass's mentula in her except by turning her back to the
beast.
(f) Isidorus (Isidore of Seville) (died c. 636 AD). Author of
histories, etc. His best known work is the *Origines* (Etymo-
logies) an encyclopedia full of misconceptions, but contain-
ing many otherwise lost quotations from ancient authors.
(g) Titus Livius (59 BC-17 AD), author of *Ab Urbe
Condita*, the most complete history of Rome which has
survived. This citation is not the famous rape of the

origin of tribads (129) Phaedrus has a fable (IV, 14):

"Another asked the reason why tribads and cinedes were created. The old man thus explained: The same Prometheus, modeller of the human clay which, should it knock against Fortune, is shivered in pieces, once when he had all day long been fashioning separately those parts that modesty keeps hidden beneath a garment, to fit them presently to the bodies he had made, was unexpectedly invited to supper by Bacchus. There he imbibed the nectar in large draughts, and returned late home with unsteady foot; then what with fumes of wine and sleepiness, he joined the female parts to male bodies, and fixed male members on to the women. Thus it is we find lust indulging in depraved pleasures."

The masculine member applied to women is evidently that clitoris of such proportions in erection, that the tribads can use it like a penis; the female apparatus fitted on to man is nothing else but the posterior orifice, which itches in the case of cinedes, just as the vulva titillates women. Tribads were not wanting in the times of Tertullian; he calls them

---

Sabines, however, which occurred in about 753 BC, and was the abduction of Sabine women by Roman men. The incident here cited is the abduction of prostitutes by Sabine men, and it occurred in about 501 BC.

(129) Plato, *Symposium* (Works, Zweibrucken edition, vol. X, p. 205) imagines another origin; in the passage where he relates the celebrated fable according to which Jupiter had cut the men in halves, he says: "As to those women who are halves of women, they are not much harassed by desires after men; but are much more given to amuse themselves with women; the hetairistriai descend from that category."

frictrices (*De Pallio*, ch. 4):

"Look at those she-wolves who make their bread by the general incontinence; amongst themselves they are also frictrices."

The same author says in the *De Resurrectione Carnis* (ch. 16):

"I do not call a cup poisoned which has received the last sigh of a dying man; I give that name to one that has been infected by the breath of a *frictrix*, of a high priest of Cybele, of a gladiator, of an executioner, and I ask if you will not refuse it as you would such persons' actual kisses."

Nor was the trade of tribad out of date in the time of Luisa Sigea:

"Nay! do not think me," says Tullia, (*Dialogue* II) "worse than others. This taste is spread almost over every part of the earth. Italians ,Spaniards, French women love one another; if they were not ashamed, they would always be rutting in each other's arms."

More, she quotes herself (*Dialogue* VII) some examples of the transports of tribads:

"Enemunda, the sister of Fernando Porcio, was very beautiful, and not less so was a friend of hers, Francisca Bellina. They frequently slept together in Fernando's house. Fernando laid secret snares for Francisca; the latter knew that he desired to have her, and was proud of it. One morning the young man, stung by his desires, rose with the sun, and stepped out upon the balcony to cool his hot blood. He heard the bed of his sister in the next room creaking and shaking. The door stood open; Venus had been kind to him and had made the girls careless. He enters; they do not see him blinded and deafened by pleasure. Francisca was riding Enemunda, both naked, full gallop. 'The noblest and most powerful mentulas are every day after my maidenhead,' said Francisca, 'I should select the finest, dear, but for you; so fain am I to gratify your tastes and mine.' Whilst speaking she was jogging her vigorously. Fernando threw himself naked into the bed; the two girls, almost frightened to death, dared not stir. He draws Francisca, exhausted by her ride, into his arms and kisses her: 'How dare you, abandoned girl' he says, 'violate my sister, who is so pure and chaste? You shall pay me for this; I will revenge the injury done to our house; answer now to my flames as she has answered to yours.' 'My brother! my brother! cries Enemunda, 'pardon two lovers, and do not betray us to slander!' 'No one shall know anything,' he answered, 'let Francisca make me a present of her treasure, and I will make you both a present of my silence.'"

The conversation of Ottavia with Tullia acting as tribad, in the same work (*Dialogue* II) is still bolder and more to the point:

"*Tullia.* Pray do not draw back; open your thighs.

"*Ottavia.* Very well. Now you cover me entirely, your mouth against mine, your breast against mine, your belly against mine; I will clasp you as you are clasping me.

"*Tullia.* Raise your legs, cross your thighs over mine, I will show you a new Venus; as you are quite new at this. How nicely you obey! I wish I could command as well as you execute!

"*Ottavia.* Ah! ah! my dear. Tullia, my queen how you push! how you wriggle! I wish those candles were out; I am ashamed there should be light to see how submissive I am.

"*Tullia.* Now mind what you are doing! when I push, do you rise to meet me; move your buttocks vigorously, as I move mine, and lift up as high as ever you can! Is your breath coming short?

"*Ottavia.* You dislocate me with your violent pushing; you stifle me; I would not do it for any one but you.

"*Tullia.* Press me tightly, Ottavia, take ... there! I am all melting and burning, ah! ah! ah!

"*Ottavia.* Your affair is setting fire to mine—draw back!

"*Tullia.* At last, my darling, I have served you as a husband; you are my wife now!

"*Ottavia.* I wish to heaven you were my husband! What a loving wife I should make! What a husband I should have! But you have inundated my garden; I am all bedewed What have you been doing, Tullia?

"*Tullia.* I have done everything up to the end, and from the dark recesses of my vessel, love in blind transports has shot the liquor of Venus into your maiden barque."

Leo Africanus (h), in his *Description of Africa* (p. 336 edition Elzevir, of 1632), mentions the tribads of Fez:

"But those who have more common sense, call these women (he is speaking of witches) 'Sahacat,' a word

---

(h) Leo Africanus (c1494-c1552). Born in Granada of Moorish parents, he is known by a variety of names (Joannes Medices, Al-Hassan ibn Mohammad, and others). He travelled through North Africa and was captured by Venetians on one of his voyages to Constantinople. Converted to Christianity by Pope Leo X, he remained in Italy and in 1550 published an account of his travels.

which corresponds with the Latin *fricatrices*, because
they take their pleasure with each other. I cannot
speak more plainly without offending decency. When
good-looking women visit them, these witches fall at
once in hot love with them, not less hot than the love
of young men for girls, and they ask them in the guise
of the devil to pay them by suffering their embraces.
So it happens that very often when they think they
have been obeying the behests of demons, they have
really only had to do with witches. Many too, pleased
with the game they have played, seek of their own
impulse to enjoy intercourse again with the witches,
and under pretense of being ill, summon one of them
or send their unfortunate husbands to fetch her. Then
the witches, seeing how matters stand, swear that the
wife is possessed by a demon, and can only be liberated by joining their association."

You ask whether tribads are still to be found in our
days? If there are none now, there certainly were
some in existence in Paris only a short time before the
Great Revolution, if we are to trust the author of the
Gynaeology (III, p. 428). There was a veritable college
of tribads in Paris, who went by the names of Vestals,
holding regular meetings in particular localities. There
were a great many members, and of the highest
classes; they had their statutes with respect to admission; the affiliated were divided into three degrees:
aspirants, postulants, the initiated. Before the postu-
lant could be admitted to the secret of the order, she
had to undergo for three days a difficult probation:
shut up in a cell tapestried with lewd pictures, and
ornamented with carved Priapi of magnificent proportions, she had to keep up a fire with I do not know

how many ingredients, and arranged in such a manner
that it would go out if there was taken too much or
too little of any of the materials; on the four altars of
the temple, adorned with splendid hangings and with
statues of Sappho, of the Lesbians she had loved, and
of the Chevalier d'Eon (i), who for so many years
successfully dissimulated his sex, perpetual fires were
burning. English "kept women" too did not recoil at
Tribadism, as the same author states (III, p. 394). He
affirms that not long before the close of the last
century, confederacies of tribads, called Alexandrine
confederacies, were still in existence in London,
though in a small number only.

Enough now of those who are, strictly speaking,
included under the name of Tribads; but the word has
a more extended signification. The term is also applied
to those women who in default of a real mentula,
make use of their finger or of a leather contrivance,
which they introduce in their vulva, and so attain a
fictitious enjoyment. Germany, I have lately heard, has
been ringing with complaints about this abuse. As
regards the leather engine (130) called by the Greeks
olisbos, the women of Miletus, above all others, made
it their instrument of pleasure. Aristophanes, in the
Lysistrata (108-110):

"For since the day the Milesians left us in the lurch,
not an *olisbos* have I set eyes on, eight inches long,—
that might give us its leather aid . . ."

---

(130) Another use of these leather engines has been noted
in chap. II.
(i) Charles-Genevieve, Chevalier d'Eon de Beaumont
(1728-1810), who passed as a woman for many years.

Suidas under the word *Olisbos*:

"A virile member made of leather which was used by Milesian women, as being tribads and immodest. It was also made use of by widows."

The same author under the word *Misete*:

"Cratinus also says on this head: Lewd (*misetai*) women will be using the *olisbos*."

Hesychius quotes the same passage.

If you ask whether modern women, who have suffered the wrong of seeing their beauty slighted, actually have recourse to this leather substitute, Luisa Sigea (*Dialogue* II) shall answer you:

"The Milesian women made for themselves imitations in leather, eight inches long and thick in proportion. Aristophanes tells us that the women of his day habitually made use of such. And to this very day Italian, Spanish and Asiatic women honor this instrument with a place in their toilet apparatus; it is their most precious possession, and one very highly appreciated."

It is an undoubted fact that the Roman matrons cherished a species of inoffensive snake (131), the cold

---

(131) This sort of snake served also to amuse men. Suetonius, *Tiberius* (72): "He kept for amusement a snake; one day, when he went as usual to feed it, he found it devoured entirely by ants, which he took as a warning to guard against being attacked by a mob." Pliny, *Nat. Hist.* (XXIX, xii, 72): "The Aesculapian serpent was brought to Rome from Epidaurus; it was kept in the public edifices, and also in private houses." Seneca, in the *De Ira* (II, 31, 6), speaks of: "Those snakes that glide harmlessly amid the cups and into the bosoms of the guests." They were not of a small size; this appears from what Philostratus (k) says in his *Heroics* (VIII, i): "Ajax had at tame snake of five cubits length, which kept close to him, guided him on his way, and followed him about like a dog." This kind of snake

skin of which served as a refrigerator in summer; Martial (VII, 87):

"If Gracilla winds an icy serpent around her neck ..."

Lucian, *Alexander* (Works, vol. IV, p. 259):

"In that country one sees serpents of an enormous size, but so quiet and mild that they are fondled by women, sleep with the children, do not get angry on being trodden on or handled, and suck the nipples of the breast like a nursling."

This being so, our eminent Boettiger (j) was probably right, when he wrote page 454 of his *Sabina*, (132) a profoundly scientific work in German, that very likely snakes were used as instruments to satisfy the lubricity of amorous women. You may understand now what happened, or what might have happened to Atia, the mother of Augustus, of whom Suetonius (*Augustus*, 94) wrote:

"I read in the treatise of Asclepiades of Mendes called the *Theologumena*, how Atia the mother of Augustus, having gone at midnight to the temple of

---

was very common at Pella, in Macedonia, as Lucian says in a passage quoted in the text: "There are many such in their country." They are still to be found in Italy, according to Justus Lipsius in his Notes to Seneca.

(132) "Sabina, or the Morning Toilet of a Roman Lady at the end of the First Century," translated into French by Clapier, 1813, 8vo.

(j) Karl August Boettiger (1760-1835), an archaelogist and Latin scholar. In 1803, he published *Sabina, oder Morgenszenen in Putzzimer einer reichen Roemerin.*

(k) Flavius Philostratus the elder of Lemnos (3rd century AD) taught at Athens and Rome. He wrote *Heroicus*, biographies of the mythical heroes of the Trojan War. He also wrote a life of Apollonius of Tyana and a description of paintings.

Apollo, to assist at a solemn sacrifice, fell asleep, and
so did the other women present; how a serpent suddenly glided close to her, and after some little time
withdrew again, and how on waking she purified
herself as though she had left the arms of her husband. (l)"

There would be nothing surprising in the fact that a
serpent of that sort should have investigated even
without incitation on Atia's part, a certain locality
which was well known to it by the lubricity of other
women, and that Atia felt on awakening the very same
sensation, as though she had undergone a real coitus.

(l) Suetonius continues that 10 months later, Atia gave
birth to Augustus "and therefore he was considered to be
the son of Apollo." A similar legend is related concerning
Olympias, the mother of Alexander the Great, so that he
could claim to be the son of Zeus.

OF INTERCOURSE WITH ANIMALS

CHAPTER SEVEN

OF INTERCOURSE WITH ANIMALS.

It will not be out of place to say something here of the incontinence of those who have carried out carnal intercourse with animals. It appears that in Egypt the Mendesians, who paid divine honors to a he-goat (133), prostituted to him publicly women, even against his inclination, in celebrating his rites. Herodotus (II, 46):

"A monstrous affair was connected with this district (viz. the Mendesian) in my time; a he-goat covered a woman in public."

Strabo (a) (XVII, p. 802):

"Mendes, where they worship Pan, and a live he-goat; the latter in that place has intecourse with

---

(133) Plutarch, *Beasts Are Rational* (*Bruta Animalia ratione uti,* p. 989, vol. II, of his works): "It is reported in Egypt a he-goat at Mendes, shut up with a great number of women, all of them beautiful, refused to have anything to do with them, and prefers goats by far."

(a) Strabo (c63 BC-after 21AD) of Pontus, author of *Geographica* giving much information on the ancient world.

women (134)."

The Jews also knew something of the practice; as we know from the law of Moses, *Leviticus* (XX, 15-16):

"And if a man lie with a beast, he shall surely be put to death: and ye shall slay the beast. And if a woman approach unto any beast, and lie down thereto, thou shalt kill the woman, and the beast: they shall surely be put to death ..."

How should Juvenal have come to tell us, *Satire* VI (332-33):

" ... she will not wait an instant more but offers her buttocks to a young ass to mount her from behind," if it had not been known that women sometimes submitted themselves to asses? Would Apuleius have thought of describing to us with no less minuteness than wit the scene in which Lucius, changed into an ass by a mistake of Fotis, effects intercourse with a matron? *Metamorphoses* (book X. 227):

"But I was a prey to grave apprehensions; I asked myself how I, with my long and coarse legs, could mount a delicate woman, clasp with my hard hoofs her soft and tender limbs that looked like milk and honey; how I could with my enormous mouth, furnished with teeth as big as tomb-stones, kiss those small, rosy, scented lips; how lastly this lady, although in rut to her very finger nails, could take in such a big genital verge ... She, however, doubled her tender allurements, her endless kisses, her sweet murmurings, interspersed with sweet glances like stings: 'I hold you

---

(134) If we may believe Venette (II, iv. 3), there is nothing more common in Egypt at the present day than for young women to have intercourse with he-goats.

at last,' she cried, 'I hold my dove my sparrow!' and
having said this, she showed me how vain my fears
had been, for embracing me as closely as she could,
she received me inside entirely, out and out. Even
more than that, whenever I drew back in order to
spare her, she pushed closer to me, and clasping my
backbone like mad, she clung to me so closely that, by
Hercules, I began to think that I was not well enough
furnished to assuage her passion completely."

A young girl of Tuscany got herself covered by a
dog in the time of Pius V (b), the Roman Pope, as
reported by Venette (II, iv, ch. 3); and according to a
note of Elmenhorst on the passage of Apuleius quoted
on the previous page, a woman was discovered in
Paris, in October, 1601, to have had connection with a
dog. The law was appealed to, and in conformity with
the unanimous verdict pronounced by the parliament,
the adulterous woman and the dog were both burned
alive. Nay! more, a woman has been known to submit
to a crocodile, if we may believe Plutarch, who reports
in his treatise *The Cleverness of Animals* (*De Solertia
Animaliun*, p. 976, vol. II, of the complete Works):

"Quite lately our excellent Philinus, on returning
from a long voyage to Egypt, told me that he had seen
at Antaeopolis an old woman sleeping with a crocodile
stretched comfortably beside her on her pallet."

Nor have men despised the vulva of animals. Plate
III of the *Monuments du culte secret des dames
romaines*, shows the picture of a man working away
in a goat, though the annotator ought not to have
quoted in illustration of it a passage of Vergil (*Buco-*

(b) Pius V, pope from 1566 to 1572.

lics, III, 8), which has nothing whatever to do with this matter:

"We know who (pedicated) you, while the he-goats looked at you askance."

In our countries legal cases show that not only goats, but also sheep, cows, and mares, have sometimes charmed shepherds and other people of low breeding.

OF SPINTRIAN POSTURES

CHAPTER EIGHT

OF SPINTRIAN POSTURES

In the sundry kinds of voluptuous enjoyment which we have studied so far, there are almost always only two persons in action. It happens, nevertheless, that more than two, three or even more, may enjoy themselves together; this is what we call after Tiberius, the spintrian kind. Suetonius, *Tiberius* (43):

"In his retreat at Capri he had a *sellaria,* the scene of his secret debaucheries, in which chosen groups of young girls and worn-out voluptuaries, the inventors of monstrous conjunctions, called by him *spintries,* forming a triple chain, surrendered themselves to mutual defilements in his presence, so as to re-animate by this spectacle his languishing desires."

This *sellaria,* by the etymology of the word, was evidently a room furnished with seats; those who prostituted each other on these seats were called "*sellarii,*" from the place, and "*spintriae,*" from the chain they formed. Spinter, according to Festus (p. 443), signified, "a kind of bracelet worn by women on

the upper part of the left arm." The word is probably
a corruption of *sphincter*, the Greek *sphigkter* from
sphiggo, "I clasp" as for instance, a band surrounding
the arm. Tacitus *Annals* (VI, ch. 1):

"Then there were invented names never known
before, as for instance, *sellarii* and *spintriae*, names
taken from the turpitude of the place or from the
complicated infamies undergone."

Spintries then are those who, linked like the rings of
a bracelet, thus accomplish the pleasure of Venus.
Three can link themselves thus, two and two, in such a
way that while the middle one is a fornicator or a
pedicon, in front is a woman or a cinede, behind a
pedicon. Such was the chain formed by those Ausonius (*Epigram* CXIX) describes (135):

"Three in one bed; two submit to the infamous act,
two perform it—Four there are, I suppose.—Wrong!
to the outermost ones give a villainy apiece; count the
man in the middle twice, for he both acts and submits."

Do you want to see the one in the middle working a
woman. Plate XL of the *Monuments de la vie privée
des louze Césars* shows you an example. Do you wish
to see the middle one pedicating? look at plate XXVII.

There is, however, no need that the middle actor
should fornicate or pedicate. He may be placed between his two companions in such a way that while he

_____

(135) Translation by Ausonius of a Greek Epigram of
Strato (a), to be found in Brunck's *Analecta* (II, 380,
XCV).
(a) Strato of Sardis (early 2nd century AD), a writer of
Greek erotic poetry.

is enduring the assault of a pederast behind, he may in
front irrumate, suck a member or lick a vulva. Hostius
whose mind was so fertile in inventing obscenities that
he was held up as an example to future ages, has tried
all these postures and even added fresh variations.
Seneca (*Nat. Quaest.*, I, 16) has inveighed against him
more vehemently than is perhaps fit for a philosopher.
It seems to me as though some secret voluptuousness
had been acting here on the sense of this rigid guar-
dian of virtue; he says:

"I will tell you here a story which will show you
that lust will not disdain any artifice which is calculated to rouse desires, and to stimulate its own fury.
The lasciviousness of Hostius was of the extremest
kind. It was this rich miser, this slave of a hundred
million sesterces, whose death, when he had been
assassinated by his slaves, Augustus would not
avenge, although he would not say that they were
right to kill him. His lewdness was not contented with
one sex; he was as passionate for men as for women.
He had mirrors made which magnified the reflections
so much that a finger appeared as big as an arm.
These mirrors were placed in such a manner that when
he had a man under him he could watch every movement of his accomplice, and enjoy as it were the
fictitious size of his member. He chose his men carefully, the measuring tape in hand, and still had to
deceive his insatiable passion. It would be too outra-
geous to report everything which this monster, who
ought to have been torn into pieces, dared to say and
do with his mouth; when surrounded on all sides by
his mirrors he was the spectator of his own turpitudes,
and those secret infamies which every man would

deny, if accused of them. Of such he took his fill not
with his mouth only, but also with eyes. And, by
Hercules, generally speaking crimes shun their own
reflection; men who are bare of every feeling of honor
and exposed to every insult, still have some sense of
shame, and do not like to appear as they are. But he
feasted his eyes on unheard of and unknown infamies,
and, not content to see simply how he dishonored
himself, he surrounded himself with mirrors, for the
sake of multiplying and grouping his lubricities. As he
could not see unaided everything dstinctly when, pedicated by one man, he had his head between the
thighs of another, he saw by his mirrors what he was
doing and how. He saw the lewd work of his mouth,
and watched himself absorbing men by every orifice.
Sometimes placed between a man and a woman,
playing both ways the passive part, he was able to see
the greatest abominations. Darkness was not for him!
So far from being afraid of the light of day he wanted
it for his monstrous copulations, and was proud to
have them illuminated by it. Nay, more, he even
wanted to be painted in these attitudes. Even prostitutes have a certain reserve, and those that abandon
themselves to the outrages of all, veil to some extent
their poor complaisances, and the very brothel keeps
some relics of decency; but this monster turned his
obscenities into a spectacle for himself.

'Yes,' he said, 'I submit myself to a man and a
woman at the same time; but nevertheless with the
organs which are left free to me I am still able to
commit a worse ignominy. All my limbs are polluted;
then shall my eyes also take part in my enjoyments,

they shall be witnesses and judges. What I cannot see
in a natural way let me see by the help of art, so that I
may not be ignorant of what I am doing. No matter to
me that Nature has provided man with such
insignificant organs of voluptuousness, the same Nature which has furnished animals so well; I find means
to deceive my passion, and to satisfy myself. Where is
the harm, if I try to imitate nature? I will have mirrors
which shall reflect images of incredible dimensions. If
I could, I would make these images real; as I cannot, I
must be satisfied with phantoms. Let me see these
objects of obscenity larger than they are in reality, and
surprise myself by the sight of them!' The Fates were
too indulgent! This man perhaps met his doom suddenly and painlessly: he ought to have been assassinated in front of his mirrors and thus compelled to
witness his own death agony."

Plate XXI of the *Monuments de la vie privée des
douze Césars* shows the picture of Tiberius in a very
strange spintrian posture, which however is not without charm; the Emperor, half reclining on his back,
licks one girl's privates who is kneeling over him,
while he offers his penis to be sucked by another.

There are also arrangements where more than three
can join, making thus a longer chain. Let a man put
his member into a woman while both of them are
being pedicated at the same time, and you have four
people forming a triple chain, like those of Tiberius in
the passage of Suetonius previously quoted. Suppose
then another pedicon on each end, and then you have
a group of six, forming a quadruple interweaving.
Martial (XII, 43):

"There are to be found novel figures of Love, such as the impassioned fornicator may try, such as experinced libertines perform and keep the secret of; how five can copulate in a group, how more still may be connected in a chain."

Look at Plate XXXVI of the *Monuments de la vie privée des douze Césars*, with a group of five copulators artistically diversified. Nero, lying face downwards, enters one girl who is on her back, at the same time licking the privates of another who is standing; he himself is being pedicated, while the girl standing also submits her behind to a pedicon. That such a chain may be extended infinitely, is self evident.

THE END